D1639577

This book
be renew
date, auth

Glasgow
Libraries,
names f(

WHO DO YOU SAY
I AM?

Also by Jennifer Rees Larcombe

Turning Point

Unexpected Healing

Where Have You Gone, God?

WHO DO YOU SAY I AM?

The Many Names of Jesus

EVA CHAMBERS

&

JENNIFER REES LARCOMBE

Hodder & Stoughton
LONDON SYDNEY AUCKLAND

Copyright © 2000 by Eva Chambers and Jennifer Rees Larcombe

First published in Great Britain in 2000

The right of Eva Chambers and Jennifer Ress Larcombe to be identified
as the Authors of the Work has been asserted by them in accordance with
the Copyright, Designs and Patents Act 1988.

10 9 8 7 6 5 4 3 2 1

British Library Cataloguing in Publication Data
A record for this book is available from the British Library

ISBN 0 340 75621 7

Typeset in Monotype Fournier by
Strathmore Publishing Services, London N7

Printed and bound in Great Britain by
Clays Ltd, St Ives PLC

Hodder and Stoughton Ltd
A Division of Hodder Headline plc
338 Euston Road
London NW1 3BH

Contents

Acknowledgments   vii

Foreword   xi

Introduction   xvii

Jesus   1

The Anointed One   7
    Christ   8
    Friend   15

God with Us   21
    Immanuel   22

The Healer   27
    Divine Physician   28
    Suffering Servant   33

I Am Who I Am   41
    The Bread of Life   42
    The Light of the World   48
    The Good Shepherd   55
    The Vine   61

King of Kings   69

Lamb of God   77

Lord   85

Prince of Peace	95
Redeemer	105
Saviour	113
Two in One	123
Son of God and Son of Man	124
God	133

Acknowledgments

While every effort has been made to contact the copyright holders of material used in this book, this has not always been successful. Full acknowledgment will gladly be made in future editions.

We gratefully acknowledge the following, extracts from which appear in this book:

Page xvii: Peter Lewis, *The Glory of Christ*, copyright © 1992 Hodder and Stoughton.

Pages 9, 23, 125: Catherine Bramwell-Booth, *Fighting for the King*. Reproduced by permission of Hodder and Stoughton Ltd.

Page 16: Martin Smith, 'What a Friend I've Found', copyright © 1998 Curious? Music UK. Words used with kind permission of Furious? Records.

Page 15: copyright © Walther J. Mathams (1853–1931).

Pages 17, 36, 91, 126: Julian of Norwich, *Revelations of Divine Love*, copyright © 1987 Halcyon Backhouse and Rhona Pipe. Reproduced by permission of Hodder and Stoughton Ltd.

Pages 12, 51: Corrie ten Boom, *The Hiding Place*, copyright © 1971. Reproduced by permission of Hodder and Stoughton Ltd.

Acknowledgments

Page 58: John Blakesley, *Paths of the Heart – Prayers of Medieval Christians*, copyright © 1993 SPCK.

Page 62: copyright Anne Shells.

Pages 73, 81: Robert Cullinan, taken from *His Name is Jesus*, copyright © Zondervan Corporation. Used by permission of Zondervan Publishing House.

Page 97: Bishop Morris Maddocks, *A Healing House of Prayer*, copyright © 1987. Reproduced by permission of Hodder and Stoughton Ltd.

Page 125: William J. Gaither, *Because He Lives*, copyright © 1971 Kingsway's Thankyou Music.

While no direct quotations have been used, acknowledgment is also made for the following:

William Barclay, *Jesus as They Saw Him*, copyright © 1962, 1991 SCM Press.

Mary Batchelor, *Opening up the Bible*, copyright © 1993 Lion.

The editors would also like to thank Birmingham Bible Institute and Raglan Road Christian Fellowship, Smethwick, for the use of their libraries in research for this book.

Foreword

'Who was Jesus anyway?' a twelve-year-old friend asked me recently. There was no time to answer him then so I promised to write him a letter, and this is what I said:

God is Love.

Love needs someone to love – it can't exist in a vacuum. It has to express itself to the object of its love and to have that love returned.

So God created human beings, and a perfect Earth environment, in which they could live. They were there to be his companions and he wanted to be there for them too, in a relationship of perfect love, mutual trust and enjoyment.

But he also gave them the greatest gift of all, the freedom to choose or reject his love. He didn't programme them like robots to return his love automatically because no one wants to be loved when there is no alternative. Real love has to be given voluntarily.

Sadly, right from the start most humans chose not to trust him, love him or observe his ten rules for happiness.

They decided to 'do their own thing', 'play it their way', 'look after number one' and all the other age-old clichés that have systematically destroyed the peace and happiness of humankind down the ages.

Because God is Love, it was impossible for him to

abandon the people he loved so much – even when they chose to ignore him. So he set about trying to let them know the extent of his love.

He sent them messages through his personal friends the prophets, but no one would listen. He spoke direct from Mount Sinai but those who heard his voice were so terrified they pleaded never to hear it again.

He communicated via impressive angels but people dismissed them as imaginary.

So God decided to come to earth himself – in person – to talk to us directly. He didn't only come to tell us he loved us. He had another reason.

Because God is Love, love is his highest priority and he can't stand it when one human fails to love another as much as he loves himself. Doing this leads to envy, stealing, lying, violence, killing, lack of respect for the old and ill and lack of commitment to marriage and family. These failures of love always hurt someone – usually the weak and vulnerable – so, because justice for the helpless matters vitally to God, those who hurt other people have to be punished.

But every human being is basically selfish, so fair punishment meant wiping out the whole human race. How could Love possibly do that? Love couldn't – but Love could take the punishment in their place. So God came to earth to demonstrate his love by dying in our place.

If he had appeared in all his thunderous, terrifying glory, people would have fainted with fright, so he came in a human body. The essence of divine power and personality were joined to a human ovum, which burrowed into the walls of an ordinary uterus and developed into a baby. The child grew up in a country village, one of a large family, and became an ordinary manual worker. He never travelled far from home, went to university, wrote a book, led an army, formed a government or accepted high-ranking office. He spent his time with the disabled, the misfits, the no-hopers and failures. Because he showed them what love really is, he gave them back lost hope and self-respect. He mended broken hearts as easily as he mended broken limbs and he set free those who were trapped in prisons of anger, despair and guilt.

And the religious people hated him for it. 'He says he can forgive sin,' they argued, 'but only God can do that! And he says he was alive before Abraham, so he must either be a dangerous lunatic or the most evil man on earth. We must kill him to protect ourselves from the results of such wicked lies.' So they flogged him, nailed him to a cross and left him to die in agony.

Of course he could easily have kicked them all out of the universe, but he didn't. He stayed on that cross because it was the only way to bring justice to the oppressed and to save the oppressors from the consequences of their selfishness.

After three days, buried in a tomb, he was up and off again, caring for a broken-hearted prostitute, a friend who had betrayed him three times over and a group of unsuccessful fishermen.

After forty days, his human body was seen returning to heaven by many witnesses but his spirit returned to live in the bodies of those who choose to love and follow him. When every human being has had a chance to make that all-important choice between light and darkness, good and evil, he will appear again and rule the world in perfect love and justice.

This is Jesus, God and Man combined, King of the Universe.

◄◄--►►

When I was asked by Eva Chambers and Hodder and Stoughton to help write a book about Jesus, I was initially rather nervous. I am no theologian!

'We want this book to be a collection of some of the things people have written about Jesus over the last two thousand years,' they said. 'Little snippets from people who have known and loved him in many different circumstances.' It was then that I began to catch the excitement.

'You mean a jigsaw puzzle of words,' I said. 'Each piece on its own just a fragment of the truth, but when they are all slotted together they create a complete picture! But how can I help?'

They went on to explain that Eva had collected a beautiful selection of historical writings, but that they felt it was important not just to give the views of famous people from the past. They wanted to show what Jesus means to people nowadays. Not the leading, well-known Christians, but 'ordinary' people. They asked me to hunt out a selection of such people – from various backgrounds and denominations – and ask them why they believe Jesus is alive today and what he means to them, personally.

It sounded an interesting commission for a writer like myself, but it has turned out to be far more than that. In fact it would be hard to explain just how much I have gained from it on a personal level. My search for these 'ordinary' people has taken me all over the country, into a prison, a primary school, a carpenter's shop, a Fellow's study in an Oxford college, a plush London office, a hospital, an army barracks, a doctor's surgery and the cluttered pad of a university undergraduate. I feel my faith has been greatly enriched by the experience of looking at Jesus through their eyes and discovering what difference a man born two thousand years ago can make to ordinary lives today.

You will find their stories – which I have encouraged them to tell in their own words – at regular intervals throughout the book.

The experiences of these people fit so well with the jigsaw pieces from the past that Eva has carefully collected that I feel this book does give a very vivid and living picture of Jesus, seen as he is, from so many different angles. Perhaps the finished jigsaw is not the old-fashioned flat kind but one of those new, three-dimensional 'jigsaw sculptures' that only the most patient people ever attempt! The pieces are certainly not made of cardboard or wood; they are each fashioned from 'treasures of darkness' (Isaiah 45:3), precious stones which are only discovered in the dark mines of the soul where faith is the only light and love the final product.

JENNIFER REES LARCOMBE

Introduction

There is a story I read recently, recounted by the theologian Peter Lewis. It tells of a preacher who, when aged about twelve, had a great hero. This hero was a sportsman who gained a cap in rugby for playing for his country, and who played cricket to county standard.

Two years later, he actually got to know his hero personally. They were both keen anglers and used to go fishing together. On these occasions the preacher was able to observe him from an entirely different viewpoint and got to know the man and not merely the image. But he became very disillusioned as he discovered the true character of the man whose public image had so captivated him.

'The nearer I got, the smaller he became,' he said. But then he added: 'God eventually led that downcast schoolboy to a new hero. And I have walked with my Jesus for thirty-five years now. In that time I have often disappointed him, but he has never disappointed me! I have got to know him better, and the nearer I get the bigger he becomes!'

That preacher's experience has also been mine. In putting together this book, I moved a lot closer to Jesus. I thought there would come a time when I got a 'handle on him' – a time when I thought, 'yes, that's all there is on his names'. But that time never came. Just when I thought I had encapsulated everything about him on paper and the smaller he was supposed to become, the more there was to find out about him and the bigger he became!

As a result, this book is far from exhaustive – there are many more names of Jesus, many more treasures written in worship of him, many more real-life experiences. What I hope Jennifer and I have done is to give a glimpse into the character of Jesus and to inspire you to deepen your relationship with him – whether that means getting to know him better or inviting him into your heart for the first time.

The names of Jesus, to me, are like the facets of a diamond. They illuminate both his humanness and divine qualities, just like the nicknames and familiar names we are known by often show our true natures. The most amazing thing is that while our names sometimes show the sinful side to us, the names of Jesus reveal that he is completely good, beautiful and true.

There is no hidden bad side to Jesus, and the eighteen names detailed in this book go some way to proving that fact. If Jesus is all good, then his Father must be all good too, and we can trust him with every part of our lives. He will never disappoint us, even though we, like the preacher in the story, often disappoint him.

I pray that you will enjoy *Who Do You Say I Am?* and that through it you will catch sight of how big God really is!

EVA CHAMBERS

Jesus

> She will give birth to a son, and you are to give
> him the name Jesus, because he will save his
> people from their sins.
>
> — MATTHEW 1:21

*The name Jesus wasn't chosen by accident. Despite it being a
very ordinary name for the time, it had special significance for
those who would come to know him. For many, the name is used
as a curse, with little thought for its true meaning. But in
the language of the Jews — Hebrew — the name Jesus means
Saviour. And in the Greek language Jesus means the Healer. So
Jesus was predestined to rescue people from the grip of sin, and
to cure diseased bodies and souls. It could be no other way.*

> Jesu is in my heart, his sacred name
> Is deeply carved there: but th'other week
> A great affliction broke the little frame.
> Ev'n all to pieces: which I went to seek:
> And first I found the corner, where was J,
> After, where E S, and next where U was graved.
> When I had got these parcels, instantly
> I sat me down to spell them, and perceived
> That to my broken heart he was I ease you,
> And to my whole is JESU.

> — GEORGE HERBERT

There is a name all names above,
Exalted name of Jesus;
It tells us of a Father's love,
The saving name of Jesus;
It is the sinner's only plea,
The seal of his salvation;
It is the Christian's joyful hope,
His faith's secure foundation.

There is a name where in we hide,
The fortress-name of Jesus,
The refuge where our souls may bide,
The mighty name of Jesus;
It was our fathers' dwelling place
And still for us availing;
Unshaken should its ramparts stand
Against the world's assailing.

There is a name by which we live,
The one great name of Jesus,
And daily triumph it will give,
The Victor-name of Jesus;
It is the sword that smites our foes
With lightning stroke of splendour,
For every danger, every fear,
Our shield and our defender.

— ANNIE JOHNSON FLINT

As honey to the taste, as melody in the ear, as songs of gladness in the heart, so is the name of Jesus. And medicine it is as well ... Naught but the name of Jesus can restrain the impulse of anger, repress the swelling of pride, cure the wound of envy, bridle the onslaught of luxury, extinguish the flame of carnal desire – can temper avarice, and put to flight impure and ignoble thoughts. For when I name the name of Jesus, I call into mind at once a man meek and lowly of heart, benign, pure, temperate, merciful; a man conspicuous for every honourable and saintly quality; and also in the same person the Almighty God – so that He both restores me to health by His example and renders me strong by His assistance. No less than this is brought to my mind by the name of Jesus whenever I hear it.

– ST BERNARD OF CLAIRVAUX

The noble love of Jesus impels man to do great things, and stirs him up to be always longing to be more perfect.

– ST THOMAS À KEMPIS

Jesus! Who deemst it not unmeet
To wash Thine own disciples' feet,
Though Thou wert Lord of All;
Teach me thereby this wisdom meek,
That they who self-abasement seek
Alone shall fear no fall.

– F.W. FABER

How sweet the name of Jesus sounds
In a believer's ear;
It soothes his sorrows, heals his wounds,
And drives away his fear.

It makes the wounded spirit whole,
And calms the troubled breast;
'Tis manna to the hungry soul,
And to the weary rest.

– JOHN NEWTON

If there is one name sweeter than any other, it is the name Jesus. Jesus! It is the name that moves the harps of heaven to make beautiful melody. Jesus! It is woven into the very fabric of our worship. Many of our hymns begin with it, and hardly any, if they're worth anything, end without mentioning it. It is the sum total of all delights. It gathers up all the hallelujahs of eternity in just five letters. Jesus!

– CHARLES SPURGEON

The Anointed One

CHRIST

> The woman said, 'I know that Messiah' (called Christ) 'is coming. When he comes, he will explain everything to us.' Then Jesus declared, 'I who speak to you am he.'
>
> —JOHN 4:25–26

Jewish people in Bible times considered themselves specially chosen by God. They suffered a great deal and so were watching out for a divine figure who would bring them honour and glory. But when Jesus actually arrived – who was the Christ, or Messiah – they managed to miss him! Instead of accepting him as who he was, they rejected him and finally crucified him. But what could have been the most terrible mistake in history led to an incredible U-turn. For the Messiah, the Anointed One, rose from the dead. And by doing so he brought honour not only to the Jews, but to all those who believed then and who believe today.

When Jesus came to Bethlehem
To guide men,
To be a star and son for them,
New light came down for me there,
New light for sinners everywhere,
When Jesus came to Bethlehem.

When Christ was born in Bethlehem
To save men,
To live and die and rise for them,
New hope was born for me there,
New hope for sinners everywhere,
When Christ was born in Bethlehem.

When God appeared in Bethlehem
To love men,
To save and keep and comfort them,
New peace was found for me there,
New peace for sinners everywhere.
New light, new hope, new peace for thee,
New light, new hope, new peace for me
For always,
For this day and every day,
Since God appeared in Bethlehem.

— CATHERINE BRAMWELL-BOOTH

Who Do You Say I Am?

For unto us a Child is born, unto us a Son is given: and the government shall be upon His shoulder; And His Name shall be called Wonderful Counsellor, the Mighty God, the Everlasting Father, the Prince of Peace.

– ISAIAH 9:6

I believe, O merciful Jesus, that thou art Christ the true Messiah, the anointed of the Lord, the promised seed, 'which was to bruise the serpent's head', long expected by the fathers, foretold by the prophets, represented by types, which were all fulfilled in thee, O thou the desire of all nations: all love, all glory, be to thee.

– THOMAS KEN, BISHOP OF BATH AND WELLS
(1637–1711)

Name him, brothers, name him,
With love as strong as death,
But with awe and wonder,
And with bated breath;
He is God the Saviour,
He is Christ the Lord,
Ever to be worshipped,
Trusted and adored.

– CAROLINE M. KNOWLE

Sleep, Holy Babe!
While I with Mary gaze
In joy upon that face awhile,
Upon the loving infant smile,
Which there divinely plays.

Sleep, Holy Babe!
Ah! Take Thy brief repose:
Too quickly will Thy slumbers break,
And Thou to lengthen'd pains awake,
That death alone shall close.

Then must these hands
Which now so fair I see;
These little dainty feet of Thine
So soft, so delicately fine,
Be pierced and rent for me!

Then must that brow
Its thorny crown receive;
That cheek, more lovely than the rose,
Be drench'd with blood, and marr'd with blows,
That I thereby may live.

— E. CASWALL

Who Do You Say I Am?

Christ my king, I want you and you alone as my Lord and Lord of everyone. You have redeemed us, given yourself as ransom for my sin, and the sin of all the world. You have delivered us from the power of evil.

— JOHN BESSARION

His likeness to Christ is the truth of a man, even as the perfect meaning of a flower is the truth of a flower ... As Christ is the blossom of humanity, so the blossom of every man is the Christ perfected in him.

— GEORGE MACDONALD

> Christ be with me, Christ within me,
> Christ before me, Christ beside me.
> Christ to win me,
> Christ to comfort and restore me,
> Christ beneath me, Christ above me,
> Christ in quiet, Christ in danger,
> Christ in hearts of all that love me,
> Christ in mouth of friend and stranger.

— ATTRIBUTED TO ST PATRICK

Jesus – The Most Important Figure in History

MY name is Sarah and I am a Fellow of an Oxford College. As a professional historian I spend my time teaching, researching and thinking about the past. If there is one thing in my professional field of which I am sure, it is that Jesus is the most important person in human history. More than any other figure from the past, Jesus has shaped the course of history. When one looks back over the last two millennia, names like Karl Marx or Christopher Columbus stand out but neither come near to the impact that Jesus has had on the formation of social, political and economic cultures. As one examines the writing of contemporaries in many different historical periods, over and over again one finds evidence of individuals who were transformed by an encounter with Jesus. Some of these individuals became world-changers who literally precipitated the rise and fall of nations; men like Martin Luther, and John Wesley. Most, however, rarely find their way into the history books. Nonetheless it is these forgotten people who form the backbone of nations.

Take Miss Weber, for example. I was reading

through a tedious pile of papers in an obscure south London archive, when Miss Weber completely took my breath away! Her memory survives only in the documented reminiscences of an elderly man, Stan Hall, who grew up in one of the roughest and most violent boroughs of London. Miss Weber was his Sunday school teacher and the only light that seems to have penetrated what was, otherwise, a monotonous and joyless existence. From a wealthy middle-class family, Miss Weber made her home in a slum court and devoted her life to telling the children of the area about Jesus. Her fiancé had been killed in the First World War and, having given up the hope of having a family of her own, she opened her tiny one-bedroom flat to 'urchins' like Stan Hall and told them Bible stories that he recalled vividly right to the end of his long life. Women like Miss Weber quietly changed communities. They did so because of the on-going impact of Jesus on human history.

As an historian I never cease to be amazed that the record of such unlikely people testifies to the continuing historical impact of Jesus. Moreover, they remind me of how Jesus is able, not only to transcend our earthly existence, but also to give it meaning and purpose in the context of history.

FRIEND

A man of many companions may come to ruin, but there is a friend who sticks closer than a brother.

— PROVERBS 18:24

When we are lonely it isn't being part of a crowd that eases the pain. We need an understanding friend and Jesus is the one who 'sticks closer than a brother'. When all the fair-weather friends have deserted us, Jesus will always be there — whispering words of comfort into our ears and holding us tightly. Jesus is also the friend of the friendless — the homeless, murderers and traitors. Those who have been shunned by society are welcomed into those loving arms.

Jesus, Friend of little children,
Be a friend to me;
Take my hand, and ever keep me
Close to thee.

— WALTHER J. MATHAMS

Who Do You Say I Am?

What a friend I've found
Closer than a brother
I have felt your touch
More intimate than lovers

Jesus, Jesus
Jesus, friend forever

What a hope I've found
More faithful than a mother
It would break my heart
To ever lose each other.

– MARTIN SMITH

The highest proof of true friendship, and one great source of its blessedness, is the intimacy that holds nothing back, and admits the friend to share our inmost secrets. It is a blessed thing to be Christ's servant; His redeemed ones delight to call themselves His slaves. Christ had often spoken of the disciples as His servants. In His great love our Lord now says: 'No longer do I call you servants'; with the coming of the Holy Spirit a new era was to be inaugurated.

– ANDREW MURRAY

It is a friendship based on the new life created in us, which has no affinity with our old life, but only with the life of God life. It is unutterably humble, unsulliedly pure, and absolutely devoted to God.

— OSWALD CHAMBERS

Thanks be to thee,
Lord Jesus Christ,
For all the benefits
Which thou hast won for us,
For all the pains and insults
Which thou hast borne for us.
O most merciful Redeemer, friend and brother,
May we know thee more clearly,
Love thee more dearly,
And follow thee more nearly,
Day by day.

— RICHARD OF CHICHESTER

It was at that time that the Lord gave me a spiritual understanding of the warm friendliness of his love. I saw that he is everything which is good and comfortable. He is our clothing: out of love for us he wraps us around, fastens the clasp, and enfolds us in his love, so that he will never leave us. I saw that he is everything that is good for us.

— JULIAN OF NORWICH

What a friend we have in Jesus,
All our sins and griefs to bear!
What a privilege to carry
Everything to God in prayer!
O what peace we often forfeit,
O what needless pain we bear,
All because we do not carry
Everything to God in prayer!

Have we trials and temptations?
Is there trouble anywhere?
We should never be discouraged:
Take it to the Lord in prayer.
Can we find a friend so faithful,
Who will all our sorrow share?
Jesus knows our every weakness:
Take it to the Lord in prayer

Are we weak and heavy-laden,
Cumbered with a load of care?
Jesus only is our refuge:
Take it to the Lord in prayer.
Do thy friends despise, forsake thee?
Take it to the Lord in prayer;
In His arms He'll take and shield thee;
Thou will find a solace there.

— JOSEPH MEDICOTT SCRIVEN

Jesus – Makes the Difference

MY name is Sandra and I live in a wheelchair. I used to be a nurse, travelling all over Britain visiting the families of babies born with handicaps caused through spina bifida. I loved travelling, loved my special babies and loved their brave and resourceful families. MS has made an enormous difference to my life, and it is progressing so rapidly that I constantly have to adjust to a new set of limitations. Sometimes, when you are diagnosed with this kind of MS you feel like a no-hoper because there is nothing medical science can do to halt the crippling downward progression.

For me, knowing Jesus makes the difference. Instead of being isolated in this nightmare and having to face an uncertain future alone, I am constantly aware that he knows all about everything I'll ever have to go through. He's already been there! He knows what it feels like to fall down (as I often do); the cross was just too heavy for him to carry and he fell under its weight. He knows what it is to need help – not to be able to move – to be humiliated and alone. He went through all that when he was hanging on the cross.

What fascinates me most about Jesus is the difference he always made to everyone who came into contact with him. No one was ever the same again. He forgave people who were haunted by guilt; he went to supper with men no one else wanted to know; restored self-respect to street women; challenged the super-religious; healed people considered to be beyond the help of doctors; calmed storms; fed hordes of hungry people; in fact he gave hope to every no-hoper he met. He always made a difference!

He was a wonderful man who did wonderful things, but I'm aware that it is the same Jesus who is alive and with me day by day, moment by moment making the difference to a life that many would write off and see as useless. When Jesus looks at me, he doesn't see a useless cripple; he sees someone worth dying for!

I would describe Jesus as my dearest friend and closest companion. Some human friends just can't cope with my MS and they have drifted away, but Jesus is different. He promised never to leave me, not to forsake or forget about me and I know for sure that he will keep his promises. His words have enthralled and challenged me for over thirty years and the wonder of it all is that I feel as if I'm only just beginning to get to know him!

God with Us

IMMANUEL

The virgin will be with child and will give birth to
a son, and they will call him Immanuel — which
means, 'God with us.'

— MATTHEW 1:23

*Eight hundred years earlier, the prophet Isaiah predicted that
Mary would give birth to a baby boy (Isaiah 7:14). And it was
no ordinary boy, but God in human form. Today, Jesus is God
'with skin on' for millions of people around the world.*

'Father!' I cried suddenly. 'God be with you!'

His head turned toward me. The harsh overhead light
flashed from his glasses.

'And with you, my daughters,' he said.

I turned and followed the others. Behind me the door
slammed closed. And with you! And with you! Oh Father,
when will I see you next?

— CORRIE TEN BOOM

(WHOSE FATHER DIED WHILE UNDER NAZI ARREST)

The cry from that Infant's throat broke the centuries of silence. For the first time in time, God's voice could actually be heard coming from human vocal cords. Everybody should have believed, but they didn't. Strangely, they must not have realised that prophetic momentum had led to prophetic fulfilment. Most still don't. But *we* do. Immanuel has come!

— CHARLES R. SWINDOLL

He speaks in language I can understand,
His hand can reach down low to take my hand;
His eye sees far ahead and guides my feet,
Whether through desert or by waters sweet;
His arm is strong enough to bear me up,
He bids my weary soul have rest and sup;
His heart is large enough to take me in,
And for His love of me, forgive my sin.
My God is more than all that I can tell,
Holy, Eternal, yet Emmanuel!
And His will is that I, poor wayward clod,
Should in simplicity be like my God!

— CATHERINE BRAMWELL-BOOTH

Who Do You Say I Am?

> Immanuel, O Immanuel,
> Bowed in awe I worship at your feet,
> And sing Immanuel, God is with us,
> Sharing my humanness, my shame,
> Feeling my weaknesses, my pain,
> Taking the punishment, the blame,
> Immanuel.
> And now my words cannot explain,
> All that my heart cannot contain,
> How great are the glories of your name,
> Immanuel.

— GRAHAM KENDRICK

Deserted! God could separate from His own essence rather;
And Adam's sins have swept between the righteous Son and
Father.
Yea, once, Immanuel's orphaned cry His universe hath
shaken —
It went up single, echoless, 'My God, I am forsaken!'

— ELIZABETH BARRETT BROWNING

Jesus – My Wisdom

MY name is Paul, I live in Kent and commute to a banking job in London. My work involves relationship banking with high-net-worth customers which means I am trusted to handle very large sums of other people's money. It is a highly stressful job, where my integrity and good judgment are vital; but on one disastrous occasion, I made a bad mistake. At a time of severe work pressure, long hours and insufficient supervisory support I made a wrong decision which compromised the bank, my customer and myself. Suddenly I found myself facing a disciplinary hearing which would probably mean the end of my career.

As I waited for the dreaded appointment I had never felt so afraid in my life. What would my wife, children and friends think of me, when they found out I had been sacked and disgraced? What about the people at church? I needed Jesus at that moment in my life, more than I had ever needed him before, but I w too paralysed by panic to pray. Looking back no realise that Jesus came to me wearing the body Christian friend, a banking colleague. I sv thought of him, the night before those diffic views with my superiors began. We had o pray together during our lunch-breaks, and somehow I knew immediately that he was the kind of person I could trust and confide in about my wretched situation

I was too ashamed to phone him from home, so I drove out to a deserted big-store car park and, using my mobile phone, I released my agony into his listening ears. What a relief! He was gentle, uncondemning and very wise. I could have been talking to Jesus himself! He gave me some excellent advice on how to approach the interviews on the following day, urging me to be totally truthful and not try to wriggle out of any necessary punishment.

To me that night, in the lonely car park, he *was* Jesus, and he continued to help and support me during the next difficult days.

In times of severe stress, our faith cannot always reach out to an abstract, invisible, intangible Jesus. We need him to have a hand we can feel, a smile we can see and a voice we can hear. I am sure it is in those times that he comes to us through people who know and love him well. Jesus has no hands nowadays to reach out and help people in trouble, so he uses ours instead. Through making that bad mistake I learnt more about the love of God than at any other time in my life.

The Healer

DIVINE PHYSICIAN

It is not the healthy who need a doctor, but the
sick. I have not come to call the righteous, but sinners to repentance.

– LUKE 5:31

*Large crowds followed Jesus, keen to hear his teaching, but also
fascinated with the miracles he performed. The feeding of the
five thousand, calming of the storm, and water turning into
wine are perhaps the most well known. But there are also
twenty-three healings recorded in the Gospels, plus three occasions where Jesus raised people from the dead! What is even
more incredible is that Jesus continues to heal some people from
sin and sickness today. Many who suffered 'terminal' disease,
crippling injuries and disabilities from birth are living physically complete lives thanks to the power of the great physician.*

For many and great are my infirmities, many and great; but your medicine is of more power. We might well have thought your word remote from union with man and so have despaired of ourselves, if he had not been made flesh and dwelt among us ...

A great physician has come to us and forgiven all of our sins. If we prefer to be ill again, we shall not only harm ourselves but be ungrateful to that physician.

— ST AUGUSTINE

Tucked away in a quiet corner of every life are wounds and scars. If they were not there, we would need no Physician. Nor would we need one another.

— CHARLES R. SWINDOLL

Come, my Light, and illumine my darkness,
Come, my Life, and revive me from death.
Come, my Physician, and heal my wounds.
Come, Flame of divine love, and burn up the
thorns of my sins, kindling my heart with the flame of
thy love.
Come, my King, sit upon the throne of my heart
and reign there.
For thou alone art my King and my Lord.

— ST DIMITRI OF ROSTOV
(17TH CENTURY)

Thou, O Christ, art all I want,
More than all in Thee I find.
Raise the fallen, cheer the faint,
Heal the sick, and lead the blind:
Just and holy is Thy name,
I am all unrighteousness;
False and full of sin I am,
Thou art full of truth and grace.

Plenteous grace with Thee is found,
Grace to cover all my sin;
Let the healing streams abound,
Make and keep me pure within:
Thou of life the fountain art,
Freely let me take of Thee,
Spring Thou up within my heart,
Rise to all eternity.

— CHARLES WESLEY

If you will you can be cured. Deliver yourself to the physician, and he will cure the eyes of your soul and heart.

— ST THEOPHILUS OF ANTIOCH

Jesus – My Healer

M Y name is Catherine. Two years ago, I believe Jesus healed me from an illness that had lasted for twenty years. My life has been so changed since then that I still feel full of awe and wonder.

When I was fourteen years old I developed the illness ME which so disabled me that I walked with sticks and used a wheelchair. I was so ill that I even got my disability benefits handed to me without attending a medical examination, which is very unusual.

Then on 3 July 1997 Jesus intervened in my life in a completely unexpected way. I was visiting a friend when a Christian lady prayed that I'd be healed in God's time. It was only a short prayer and, after so many years of illness, I can't say I had any faith that it would be answered. After the prayer, however, I suddenly knew I was no longer disabled. The crippling pain I'd suffered for years instantly left; I was standing upright instead of stooped over and a total of fifteen ME symptoms were gone, including those to do with blood sugar levels, allergies and temperature control. It was a complete, immediate healing, as dramatic as any healing which Jesus performed in the days of the New Testament.

Everyone who knew me believed in the miracle – including my doctors – they could not deny it. Even a girl working at the local supermarket said, 'I think I'll believe in God now!' as she saw me whizzing round with a shopping trolley later that same day. Over the next few weeks I gave away my walking sticks, wheelchair and other disability aids, as I no longer needed them.

Naturally my personal miracle has boosted my faith in the fact that Jesus still heals today and, for me, it is proof beyond any doubt that 'with God all things are possible' (Matthew 19:26).

SUFFERING SERVANT

Surely he took up our infirmities and carried our
sorrows, yet we considered him stricken by God,
smitten by him, and afflicted. But he was pierced
for our transgressions, he was crushed for our
iniquities; the punishment that brought us peace
was upon him, and by his wounds we are healed.

– ISAIAH 53:4–5

*Four poems in the book of Isaiah describe the servant who
suffers for his people. At that time they were not linked with the
Messiah, but Jesus took on the servant role. The last of the servant songs (above) paints a terrible picture of his punishment
and death at the hands of the Roman authorities. Death by
crucifixion was excruciating and slow. Before nails were driven
through hands and feet, the prisoner was flogged with a metal-
tipped whip and then had to carry the cross he would later die on
to the place of execution. Few of us will undergo the torture he
did, but at some time or another, all of us will have painful
trials. Because of the undeserved agony he went through, Jesus
is able to empathise with our pain.*

Who Do You Say I Am?

Hast thou no scar?
No hidden scar on foot, or side, or hand?
I hear thee sung as mighty in the land,
I hear them hail thy bright ascendant star,
Hast thou no scar?

Hast thou no wound?
Yet I was wounded by the archers, spent,
Leaned Me against a tree to die; and rent
By ravening beasts that compassed Me; I swooned:
Hast thou no wound?

No wound? No scar?
Yet, as the Master shall the servant be,
And pierced are the feet that follow Me;
But thine are whole: can he have followed far
Who has no wound nor scar?

— AMY CARMICHAEL

Pilate handed Jesus over to his soldiers to be scourged. He
had been beaten before, but this Roman scourging was
probably the most severe. We may weep as we imagine the
blows upon his precious body. Jesus stands before you,
believer, as a mirror of agonised love. If we have ever loved
our Lord Jesus, that love must be growing now as we consider his agony – the pain he went through for us.

— CHARLES SPURGEON

Lord Jesus Christ, I adore you,
You wept over Lazarus and raised him from the dead;
I beg that I may gain eternal life,
And that you will cause to spring up within me
Your fountain of living water,
Gushing out for eternal life.

Lord Jesus Christ, I adore you,
Transfixed to the cross,
Wine and myrrh to quench your thirst:
I beg that your wound may be transformed
Into a medicine for my soul.

Lord Jesus Christ, I adore you, laid in the tomb:
May your death be life to me.

— GALLICAN FORMULARIES

Vine of heaven, thy Blood supplies
This blest cup of sacrifice;
Lord, thy wounds our healing give;
To thy cross we look and live;
Thou our life! O let us be
Rooted, grafted, built on thee.

— J. CONDER

Lord, use my hands; they are not scarred like thine;
They have not felt the torture of the cross:
But they would know upon their palms
Thy touch, without which all their work is loss.

Lord, use my hands, that some may see, not me,
But thy divine compassion there expressed,
And know thy peace, and feel thy calm and rest.

— A FIJIAN NURSE'S PRAYER

For just as he was the most tender and most pure of all people, so he was the one who suffered most deeply and intensely. He suffered for the sin of every man who is going to be saved; and grieved for every man's sorrow and desolation, with natural sympathy and love. (For just as our Lady grieved for his suffering, he also grieved for her sorrow, indeed, much more, since his was a finer nature.) As long as he was capable of suffering for us and grieved for us. Now that he is risen and is no longer subject to pain, he still suffers with us as I shall explain later.

— JULIAN OF NORWICH

It happened to you

Sometimes the pain
Seems too great to bear
And it seems like I can't
Get through to you
I'm locked in this cycle of despair.

Then something makes me open up –
A film, a book, a friend
And it all pours out
And I think you couldn't possibly understand

But slowly it dawns
Nagging, insistent,
That I must forgive
Because it happened to you.

You said 'Father, forgive them'
And I must too.
I must forgive them
Because what they did to me,
They also did to you.

– EVA CHAMBERS

Jesus – My Courage

MY name is Justyn, and I am a major in the Royal Artillery. I am writing this at my desk the day before I deploy to the Balkans for an operational tour. Over the last months I have physically and mentally prepared my soldiers and myself for what we may face. As we try and maintain a fragile peace in a war-torn country, we will see a lot of broken lives, encounter hate, violence and face many unexpected dangers. Statistically, some of us will not return.

We have trained hard for this operation. We have been taught how to react in all kinds of emergencies, learnt what to do if we are caught in a minefield and we know how to use the morphine capsules that we all keep in our jacket pockets if we are injured. My soldiers will draw some courage from this level of training and from the protection they get from their helmets, flak jackets and armoured vehicles. I will draw my courage from the bravest man who ever lived.

I have been a Christian and known Jesus Christ for many years. If I knew I would be killed on this operation, I would not be able to go. Already three soldiers have gone AWOL (absent without leave) in order to avoid this operation. When Jesus came into our world he knew he would be killed. He knew it would be an agonising and humiliating death, but he still chose to die for us. He is the Son of God, yet he loved us enough to allow himself to be treated like a common criminal and his hands to be nailed to a cross. He was perfect and blameless, yet he had enough pity for us to take the punishment for our evil. He felt pain, just as we do, yet he suffered the most brutal, agonising death on our behalf.

Tomorrow I will fly to the Balkans, knowing I will face nothing he has not already been through. His strength, his love and his selflessness will be my courage. When I consider all that he did for me, my own fears and worries seem quite insignificant.

I Am Who I Am

In the Gospel of John, Jesus describes himself in seven different ways. I am: the Bread of Life; the Light of the World; the Gate; the Good Shepherd; the Resurrection and the Life; the Way, the Truth and the Life; and the Vine.

Jesus saying 'I am' has a special significance. In the Old Testament, God told Moses that he wanted to be known as 'I am who I am' (Exodus 3:14). When Jesus later called himself by the same title, he was giving people a big clue that he was God.

THE BREAD OF LIFE

Then Jesus declared, 'I am the bread of life. He who comes to me will never go hungry, and he who believes in me will never be thirsty.'

– JOHN 6:35

A short while before making this claim, Jesus had performed one of the greatest miracles ever seen. He had taken five small barley loaves and two little fish, given thanks to God for them and somehow, this meagre offering fed the five thousand who were with him (John 6:1–15). Jesus knew how important it was not to let the people grow hungry. But the name Bread of Life has a double meaning. Not only does Jesus provide for people's physical needs, he also satisfies the spiritual hunger that exists long after cravings for food have gone away.

Jesus, Thou Joy of loving hearts,
Thou Fount of Life, Thou Light of men,
From the best bliss that earth imparts,
We turn unfilled to Thee again.

Thy truth unchanged hath ever stood;
Thou savest those that on Thee call;
To them that seek Thee Thou art good,
To them that find Thee all in all.

We taste Thee, O Thou living Bread,
And long to feast upon Thee still;
We drink of Thee, the Fountainhead,
And thirst our souls from Thee to fill.

— ST BERNARD OF CLAIRVAUX

There have been times for nearly all of us when we have
felt the truth of the angel's word, 'The journey is too great
for thee'; but have we not always found the Bread of Life
and the Water of Life ready for our sustenance? And in the
strength of that meat we have gone on, and shall go on,
even unto the Mount of God.

— AMY CARMICHAEL

'Give us this day our daily bread.' How do I pray those words, Lord? I live in the context of abundance. I simply do not worry about where my next meal will come from.

Perhaps I should pray on behalf of those who really and truly live from one meal to the next. And I do pray for them. Yet, action on their behalf is the real prayer for the poor – prayer-in-action.

I do need faith daily, Jesus, and strength and patience and wisdom and love and so much more. And real material needs too. 'Give us this day our daily babysitter.' Is that how I pray for daily bread?

Teach me, Father, a life of daily dependence upon you for all things – even for the bread that is already in the pantry. Amen.

– RICHARD FOSTER

Lord Christ, the Bread of Life, what physical bread is for the body, you are for my hungry heart. You alone can save, satisfy, and strengthen my inner being. My hunger to know you better is a sure evidence that I belong to you. My heartaches are an indication of how much I need you. Bread of Life, you satisfy my deepest needs for love, self-esteem, significance, affirmation, a reason for living, involvement in a calling that counts, an assurance that there is meaning in daily living. You can give me security no one else can provide.

– LLOYD JOHN OGILVIE

'O Lord, please have them give me a little of that toasted bread.' Immediately afterwards they passed me the plate, and I bit into the 'tasty tart'. How very delicious it was! But there was shame in my heart. Was I becoming egoistic and covetous? Was hunger going to let me down? A few minutes later, before eating our turnip soup, I prayed: 'Lord, bless this food for Jesus' sake, Amen.'

How often I had prayed those words thoughtlessly! Now they were fraught with meaning. If God's blessing rested on this food it would be enough, and it would also keep me from becoming covetous.

— CORRIE TEN BOOM

Jesus – My Life

MY name is Peter and a few years ago I nearly died. At the age of twenty-eight, soon after our marriage, I had a massive stroke that has left me so disabled that my career as a research scientist was finished. Suddenly all my hopes and plans for life disintegrated. I was left to struggle every day with things that before I had done effortlessly – dressing, eating, washing. The sports and the musical instruments I used to play were impossible for me to enjoy – and there was the wheelchair. People stared pityingly, smiled patronisingly or looked away, embarrassed. They no longer responded to me – the person – I was merely an unfortunate 'case' on wheels. Many friends just didn't want to know me any more. I hated it.

I had been brought up with a church background, but my scientific education left me sceptical about the man called Jesus who claimed to be God, performed miracles and came to life after being crucified. For the first time I found myself desperate for the real answers to the 'big' questions about life. Did God exist? If he did, why had he let these awful things happen to me? If he *didn't*, then why struggle on with such a pointless life?

I was not far from suicide when the minister of a local church visited and I angrily told him how I felt. He listened and prayed for me, and he prayed 'in the name of Jesus Christ', a phrase I had heard many times but which had meant little. A few days later I woke up and immediately realised that something profound had changed me. The anguish, anger and turmoil had gone, and in their place was a deep sense of peace that I had never known before. My logical mind reasoned that since he had prayed in the name of Jesus Christ, then Jesus Christ must have answered the prayer.

Since then the peace has never left me, and I have come to recognise it as nothing less than the presence of Jesus himself with me in all the pain and frustration of disability. The physical pain has worsened, I'm frustrated by my dependence on my wife and our parents, and I know that at any time I could have another stroke and die. Yet I can't burden people with my feelings but I can pour them all out to Jesus and *know* that he understands. I can't describe it any other way except to say that he has become my friend. I can bring my practical needs to him too, and now that I am unable to earn a living, our financial needs are often great, but he always provides.

I firmly believe that Jesus Christ is alive and well, two millennia after his birth. Meeting him stopped me taking what little life I had left and his friendship has made that life worth living again.

THE LIGHT OF THE WORLD

I am the light of the world. Whoever follows me will never walk in darkness, but will have the light of life.

– JOHN 8:12

Without light we become trapped in the shadows. Not only is it difficult to see, but humans, animals and plants lose their spark and start to wither. Corruption flourishes and good people live in fear of crime. During the Israelites' exodus from Egypt, God gave a pillar of fire to guide them in the right direction (Exodus 13:21–22). But Jesus is far more than a heavenly light bulb, illuminating the road or motorway. His light shows us the wrong paths of our hearts and reveals a right and vibrant way for us to live. And the Light of the World shines so brightly that no evil can withstand it.

Come, my Light, my Feast, my Strength;
Such a Light, as shows a feast;
Such a Feast, as mends in length;
Such a Strength, as makes his guest.

– GEORGE HERBERT

I do not ask, O Lord, that life may be
A pleasant road;
I do not ask that Thou wouldst take from me
Aught of its load;
I do not ask that flowers should always spring
Beneath my feet:
I know too well the poison and the sting
Of things too sweet.
For one thing only, Lord, dear Lord, I plead,
Lead me aright:
Tho' strength should falter, and tho' heart should bleed,
Through Peace to Light.
I do not ask, O Lord, that Thou shouldst shed
Full radiance here;
Give but a ray of peace, that I may tread
Without a fear.
I do not ask my cross to understand,
My way to see –
Better in darkness just to feel Thy Hand,
And follow Thee.
Joy is like restless day, but peace divine
Like quiet night:
Lead me, O Lord, till perfect day shall shine
Through Peace to Light.

– ADELAIDE PROCTOR

Who Do You Say I Am?

I am the light of the world the founder of the Christian religion said. What a stupendous phrase! And how particularly marvellous today when one is conscious of so much darkness in the world! Let your light shine before men, he exhorted us. You know, sometimes on foolish television or radio panels, or being interviewed, someone asks me what I most want, what I should most like to do with the little that remains of my life, and I always nowadays truthfully answer, and it is truthful, 'I should like my light to shine, even if only very fitfully, like a match struck in a dark cavernous night and then flickering out.'

– MALCOLM MUGGERIDGE

Jesus Christ;
Gladsome Light!
From the glory of the Father
Gleaming
Life and light
Is your gift to the world
Day is gone
Night has come
But night and day I want to praise
My God
For the glory of the Son
Holy heavenly blessed one
Shines through all the world.

– PHOS HILARON (ANCIENT GREEK HYMN)

On my closed eyelids the sun glimmered and blazed. 'It says', I began slowly, 'that a Light has come into this world, so that we need no longer walk in the dark. Is there darkness in your life, Lieutenant?'

There was a very long silence.

'There is great darkness,' he said at last. 'I cannot bear the work I do here.'

— CORRIE TEN BOOM
(CONVERSATION WITH NAZI OFFICER)

O only source of all our light and life,
Whom as our truth, our strength, we see and feel,
But whom the hours of mortal moral strife
Alone aright reveal!

Mine inmost soul, before Thee inly brought,
Thy presence owns, ineffable divine;
Chastised each rebel self-centered thought,
My will adoreth Thine.

With eye down-dropt, if then this earthly mind
Speechless remain, or speechless e'en depart;
Nor seek to see — for what of earthly kind
Can see Thee as Thou art? —

But, as Thou willest, give or e'en forbear
The beatific supersensual sight,
So, with Thy blessing blest, that humbler prayer
Approach Thee morn and night.

— A.N. CLOUGH

Jesus – My Shield

M Y name is Sheila and I first encountered Jesus when my family and I were caught up in the Gulf War back in 1990 and at one time became part of Saddam Hussein's infamous human shield! Peter, my husband, was a serving soldier and we were in Kuwait when Iraq invaded the country. Peter was taken at gunpoint, leaving me with my two small children, not knowing if we would ever see him alive again.

It is said that when you are in a foxhole waiting for the enemy you will find no atheists! For me, in my fear and with many tears, I began to pray, which was not something I had done before. I was not sure if anyone could hear me, and I did not really know to whom I was praying, but I found comfort from asking every evening for safety and a way out of the awful things we were struggling to survive. Our hopes were raised and smashed many times before we were once again reunited as a family back in England.

On our return from the Gulf I began to search hard for answers to my many questions about the Christian faith. I longed to know the Jesus I read about in the Bible and eventually I realised it was possible to ask him to make his home in my life.

That discovery, coupled with the relief of being safely home, made every detail of my life deeply enjoyable and the damaging results of the pressure I had experienced during my ordeal in the Gulf lay dormant for two years. Then quite suddenly it was triggered into a serious post-traumatic stress disorder that resulted in me having to spend time in a secure psychiatric hospital suffering from acute psychosis.

To me, the hospital was more like a prison, and I felt such a failure that I just lay in a defeated heap, sometimes shedding many tears and at other times too exhausted to do anything but sleep. How could this happen to me? Surely, now I had Jesus in my life things were supposed to be easy? Had I done something wrong? In my confusion I felt I was living in a war zone all over again as I struggled with the many voices which plagued me night and day. My poor husband was afraid he had lost me forever.

Because of my mental state I found it impossible to relate to people and therefore felt totally alone – well, almost alone. In a strange, distant sort of way I felt Jesus was still there with me – a tiny candle flame of light in what, otherwise, felt like intense and terrifying darkness. One night, when there was no more fight left in my body, I remember crying out to him in desperation as I collapsed in a broken heap of despair.

But he heard me, and gradually I came through

that terrible experience of darkness. I believe this is because Jesus helped me to face each new day as it came.

Perhaps difficult times are inevitable for us all – they are part of life – but with Jesus at least we do not go through them alone. I am now back to full health, but mental illness is such a terrifying experience that it hangs in the memory for a very long time. I cling to the fact that Jesus said he was the light of the world, and promised never to leave me or forsake me – however deep the darkness I may have to face.

THE GOOD SHEPHERD

I am the good shepherd. The good shepherd lays
down his life for the sheep.

– JOHN 10:11

*Jesus has often been depicted carrying young sheep under his
arm. While Western urban dwellers may find it hard to relate to
this picture, it remains as true today as when he spoke of himself as a shepherd. In biblical Palestine, shepherds didn't drive
from behind, but led from the front, so the sheep could follow.
They patiently watched over the flock, rescuing any that wan-
dered off and, in some cases, even lost their lives protecting the
sheep from bandits. In the same way, Jesus goes to all kinds of
lengths to make sure his human flock is safe. So that we can
know God, he feeds us, finds us and ultimately dies for us.*

O good shepherd, seek me out, and bring me home to Thy
fold again.

Deal favourably with me according to Thy good pleasure, till I may dwell in Thy house all the days of my life,
and praise Thee for ever and ever that Thou art there.

– ST JEROME

Who Do You Say I Am?

> Jesus, tender Shepherd, hear me,
> Bless thy little lamb tonight,
> Through the darkness be thou near me,
> Keep me safe till morning light.
>
> Through this day thy hand has led me,
> And I thank thee for thy care.
> Thou hast clothed me, warmed and fed me,
> Listen to my evening prayer.
>
> Let my sins be all forgiven,
> Bless the friends I love so well;
> Take me, when I die, to heaven,
> Happy there with thee to dwell.

— MARY D. DUNCAN

As Christians we will sooner or later discover that it is in the valleys of our lives that we find refreshment from God Himself. It is not until we have walked with Him through some very deep troubles that we discover He can lead us to find our refreshment in Him right there in the midst of our difficulty. We are thrilled beyond words when there comes restoration to our souls and spirits from His own gracious Spirit.

— PHILIP KELLER

The Lord's my Shepherd, I'll not want.
He makes me down to lie
In pastures green; he leadeth me
The quiet waters by.

My soul he doth restore again,
And me to walk doth make
Within the paths of righteousness,
E'en for his own name's sake.

Yea, though I walk in death's dark vale,
Yet I will fear none ill;
For thou art with me, and thy rod
And staff me comfort still.

My table thou hast furnishèd
In presence of my foes;
My head thou dost with oil anoint,
And my cup overflows.

Goodness and mercy all my life
Shall surely follow me;
And in God's house for evermore
My dwelling-place shall be

> – SCOTTISH PSALTER 1650
> (FROM PSALM 23)

'He restoreth my soul.' He wants to restore our souls, not only for our sake, but to enable us to help others. There are friends to help and little ones to guide into the road; and life is not a 'fold', it is a journey on a road.

– EDITH BARRETT

You are the Good Shepherd,
You laid down your life for your sheep.
I am that sheep which was lost,
And yet you graciously feed me with your body and blood.
Take me up now, and carry me on your shoulders.
What good thing will you deny me,
Since you have given me your very self?
Be my shepherd,
And I shall lack nothing
In the green pasture where you have placed me,
Until you lead me to the pastures of eternal life.

– MEDIEVAL PRAYER

All the green fields of the scriptures are for all the sheep of His pasture; none are fenced off from us. Our Lord and Saviour, the great Shepherd of the sheep, Himself led the way into these fields, as a study of His use of the Old Testament shows.

– AMY CARMICHAEL

Jesus – My Reassurance

M Y name is Violet, and according to my doctors, I will die soon. The day when the consultant first told me that I had cancer, I vividly remember looking through the window, behind his head, and noticing the way the leaves were moving on a tree in time to the September breeze. My shocked mind clung tenaciously to those leaves, refusing the words it didn't want to hear.

Once the first shock had worn off, the cycle of remissions and relapses, alternating hope and fear and the miseries of chemotherapy have all become part of our family life. Yet, looking back now, I realise just what a remarkable thing has happened to me since the day I stared at those leaves. Jesus has become more real to me than anything and anyone else in my life. He is there in the endless waiting times; waiting to see the consultant; waiting to have the next scan; waiting for results; waiting for treatment; waiting for the effects of the chemo to wear off – waiting to die. Always waiting, waiting, waiting, but I have so often sensed Jesus waiting there beside me.

He has become so important to me that, in a strange way, I am faced with a dilemma. I have an increasing longing to see Jesus and spend all my time in his presence but, as a wife, mother and grandmother I feel there is still so much I want to do and enjoy down here on Earth. I firmly believe that Jesus can and does heal people miraculously today, but so far he has chosen not to heal me.

Recently the specialist has told me that my particular cancer is incurable and I began facing the possibility of dying soon. I have to confess, in spite of my desire to be with Jesus, I felt afraid of the actual dying bit. Suddenly I sensed the presence of Jesus beside me. I felt he was holding out his hand to me in a gesture which said, 'I have come to take you to my home, hold my hand and we will go there together.' Not only is he here, with me in this weird waiting time, but he is there, ahead of me, waiting there in the future for me as well. He once said,

> Do not let your hearts be troubled. Trust in God; trust also in me. In my Father's house are many rooms; if it were not so, l would have told you. I am going there to prepare a place for you. And if I go and prepare a place for you, I will come back and take you to be with me that you also may be where I am.
>
> – JOHN 14:1–3

THE VINE

I am the true vine, and my Father is the gardener. He cuts off every branch in me that bears no fruit, while every branch that does bear fruit he prunes so that it will be even more fruitful. You are already clean because of the word I have spoken to you. Remain in me, and I will remain in you. No branch can bear fruit by itself; it must remain in the vine. Neither can you bear fruit unless you remain in me.

– JOHN 15:1–4

Why a vine? Why not a majestic oak tree? Unlike other types of wood, vine wood is useless when it isn't part of the vine. In the same way, a Christian is useless if he or she pulls away from Jesus. And unlike a tree, a vine needs savage pruning for it to produce the best fruit. Cut a tree down and it will die, but when a vine is sheared it grows back. Having things cut out of our lives is a central part of the Christian life, in order to be the best for God. While this trimming may be painful at the time, the gardener knows what he is doing.

Who Do You Say I Am?

You trod on me, God.
I know You didn't mean to
I got in the way –
Just the other day –
You trod on me, God.

It wasn't your fault
(or mine for that matter)
what a splatter
squash – flat.
You trod on me, God,
And that's that.

But how now?
I know you care, aware,
And I need to get up.
It's no fun being flat,
And I am right down,
Squashed flat.
A lot of people are
Treading on me now
So how about that?

Listen to me, get it right.
Who do you think you are? God said.
Listen, I need you as wine
You were a grape off my vine,
I pressed you flat in my vat.

Oh that's fine, I said,
That's fine.
And God said: *You can forget the pain*
And be Champagne.
Champagne? I said to God
Am I that good?
Yes, said God, *That's understood*
You're the best wine
When you are mine.

– ANNE SHELLS

Holy Lord Jesus, the heavenly Vine of God's own plant-
ing, I beseech Thee, reveal Thyself to my soul. Let the
Holy Spirit, not only in thought, but in experience, give me
to know all that Thou, the Son of God, art to me as the
true Vine.

– ANDREW MURRAY

Why does the sap flow from the vine to the branch? Simply
because the branch is joined to the vine. Then the sap flows
into it by the very law of its nature. So, being joined to our
Lord Jesus by faith, that which is His becomes ours, and
flows into us by the very law of our spiritual life. If there
were no hindrance, it would indeed flow as a river. Then
how earnestly we should seek to have every barrier
removed to the inflowing of such a gift.

– FRANCES RIDLEY HAVERGAL

Who Do You Say I Am?

God can never make us wine if we object to the fingers He uses to crush us with. If God would only use His own fingers, and make me broken bread and poured-out wine in a special way! But when He uses someone whom we dislike, or some set of circumstances to which we said we would never submit, and makes those the crushers, we object. We must never choose the scene of our own martyrdom. If ever we are going to be made into wine, we will have to be crushed; you cannot drink grapes. Grapes become wine only when they have been squeezed.

– OSWALD CHAMBERS

As on a window late I cast mine eye,
I saw a vine drop grapes with J and C
Anneal'd[1] on every bunch. One standing by
Ask'd what it meant. I (who am never loth
To spend my judgement) said, It seem'd to me
To be the bodie and the letters both
Of Joy and Charitie. Sir, you have not miss'd,
The man reply'd; It figures Jesus Christ.

– GEORGE HERBERT

_____

1 Anneal'd – enamelled

It is not merely 'with Him', but 'in Him', that we are to live; and he has told us of the two conditions upon which we may abide in Him: First, the keeping of His commandments, and His commandments are not grievous, for they are all summed up in that love which is the fulfilling of the law; and, second, the bearing of fruit, the fruit of a life of love.

– EDITH BARRETT

Jesus – My Happiness

M Y name is Mike and, until I met Jesus four years ago, I thought I was completely happy. I'm the managing director of a highly successful international company and I commute between South Africa, North America, Europe and Australia. I have a beautiful home in Britain, two cars, a lovely wife, delightful daughters. I have always enjoyed my job immensely. I love the buzz I get from flying off on a challenging business trip and the sheer thrill of making a lot of money. And I'm good at doing that. When my wife began going to church I felt she was rocking our perfectly organised 'boat' and I resented it tremendously. I just couldn't understand what she saw in all that Jesus stuff. I knew God existed and I said my prayers – but why did she have to get enthusiastic about religion? Wasn't I giving her all she needed? So I refused to let her go.

Then one day a friend I respected in the business world asked me to go with him to something he called an *Alpha* course. He said I might want to discover more about who Jesus really was – I didn't – but I wanted him to think I was an open-minded kind of person, so I went with him.

The second evening something happened to me as the man at the front began to talk about Jesus. I felt I met him – himself – in person. It was a very weird feeling. I knew he was there, standing right in front of me – as real as if I could see him. I was so stunned, I handed myself over to him right then and there and gave him all I have and all I am. You see, I'm an all-or-nothing man. If Jesus is alive, and really is who he says he is, then he deserves everything – not just a bit of my time, energy and money, but all of it. I've never been the same man since!

I was always a very aggressive man – you have to be a 'hard man' to make your mark in business these days. I didn't care about treading on people's toes, but Jesus has totally softened my heart. All my life I've been going full speed towards the goal of success and making money, and I achieved that goal too. But now everything I once thought was so important I've discovered is nothing but rubbish really.

I thought happiness came from owning big cars, living in a beautiful home, enjoying fabulous holidays with lots of money to spend. I certainly enjoyed all that but now, suddenly, I'm intoxicated by Jesus. Being with him and the people who love him is a far richer kind of happiness than I've ever known before. I want to get out of the business world; it's lost all its attraction for me. In the past I never seemed to notice people who are having a hard time, I was just too busy enjoying myself, but now I want Jesus to use all the resources that I have to help people. What an adventure! Honestly, I've never felt so happy in my life.

King of Kings

On his robe and on his thigh he has this name written: KING OF KINGS AND LORD OF LORDS.

– REVELATION 19:16

While many kings rule with force and weapons, the difference with Jesus was that he ruled with love. There was a very real temptation for him to live up to the expectation of the people, and be the kind of king they wanted. After all, they were after a warrior Messiah, someone who would overthrow the enemies of Israel and take up a throne of power. But he never gave in, and the result is that his kingdom is immortal.

King of Kings! And Lord of Lords!
Thus we move, our sad steps timing
To our cymbals' feeblest chiming,
Where Thy house its rest accords.
Chased and wounded birds are we,
Through the dark air fled to Thee:
To the shadow of Thy wings,
Lord of Lords, and King of Kings!

– H.H. MILMAN

Lord Jesus, I find you throned in my heart. It is enough. I know you are enthroned in heaven. My heart and heaven are one.

— ANON

A Better Resurrection

My life is like a broken bowl,
A broken bowl that cannot hold
One drop of water for my soul
Or cordial in the searching cold:
Cast in the fire the perished thing;
Melt and remould it, till it be
A royal cup for Him, my King:
O Jesus, drink of me.

— CHRISTINA ROSSETTI

God made Jesus king over you, because He loved you, and that with nothing less than the love wherewith He loved Him. Which is the more wonderful — the love that devised such a gift, or the gift that was devised by such love! Oh, to realise the glorious value of it! May we, who by His grace know something of God's gift of His Son as our Saviour, learn day by day more of the magnificent preciousness of His gift of His Anointed One as King!

— FRANCES RIDLEY HAVERGAL

> Let all the world in every corner sing,
> My God and King!
> The heavens are not too high,
> His praise may thither fly:
> The earth is not too low,
> His praises there may grow.
> Let all the world in every corner sing,
> My God and King!
>
> Let all the world in every corner sing,
> My God and King!
> The church with psalms must shout,
> No door can keep them out:
> But, above all, the heart
> Must bear the longest part.
> Let all the world in every corner sing,
> My God and King!
>
> — GEORGE HERBERT

We are not all alike nor in the majority. We never will be! But neither are we an insignificant, struggling handful of nobodies stumbling and groping our way through life. We may be overlooked, but we're not overwhelmed. We may be unknown, but we're not unnoticed. We may be outnumbered, but we're not outclassed. We may be hidden, but we're not lost. Never forget, we're the ones who belong to the King.

— CHARLES R. SWINDOLL

Those dread words 'Laid aside' are never for us; we are
soldiers of the King of kings. Soldiers are not shelved.

— AMY CARMICHAEL

Crown of thorns and staff of spite,
Must you mock our Sovereign's might?
Know you not whom Pilate brings?
Jesus Christ, the King of Kings!

Road of sorrow, lead the way
To redeeming love today.
Let me see my Saviour's face;
Let me taste this gift of grace.

— ROBERT CULLINAN

Jesus – My Future

M Y name is Richard, I am twenty-one and in my final year at university studying aeronautical engineering. I think it would be true to say that while I've been here at Southampton I have become fascinated by Jesus. No one has ever marked history so indelibly as the carpenter from Nazareth. Who else has had so many books and songs written about them, drawings, paintings and sculptures created to portray them, buildings and monuments constructed in their honour? Who else has defined the world's calendar with their life?

What interests me most about Jesus, however, is what he said about himself. He made enormous claims that were either true, or tremendously arrogant and deceitful. Some people I meet here at university say that Jesus was just a good man and not the Son of God as he claimed. However, I cannot understand how 'just a good man' could lie so blatantly or be so revered if he was mentally ill. I believe Jesus was who he claimed to be and therefore deserves his place as the pivot of human history.

People here often ask me what Jesus means to me personally and why I bother to spend so much time with him. To me he is far more than just a historical character. His death means that I can know God, the Creator of the universe, personally. My relationship with God is the most wonderful and precious thing in my life, and it's something I did nothing to achieve or earn. Jesus died for me, that is why I love him so much.

I believe Jesus showed mankind, through his life and his death, what love really is. He loved everyone without discrimination and yet spoke very strongly against all the injustice he saw. I want to be like him, but that's not something I can just decide to do through my own hard work. Thankfully Jesus has promised to help me in my weakness.

At my age and stage in life I suppose it's normal to spend time thinking about what's important to you personally and what you want to do with your life. Now I am in my final year I am exploring career opportunities, facing interviews and making other important, life-shaping decisions. The question I am asking myself is this: is it enough simply to be fascinated by Jesus? How much am I prepared to allow him to impact and shape my future life? Is he going to be someone I visit on Sunday mornings (if I'm not too tired after a pressured week at work)? Or, when I leave here and go out into the world, is he going to be the centre of my existence and the force which drives me in the direction he has already chosen for me? He died a brutal death for me. A week later he showed his disciples his scars and then said to them, 'As the Father has sent me, so I am sending you.' Following Jesus in today's materialistic world will be costly; I may not have to die on a cross for him, but there may be other difficult things to live through. However, for me, meeting Jesus face to face in heaven one day will be worth everything I could ever give up for him down here on earth.

Lamb of God

> The next day John saw Jesus coming towards him and said, 'Look, the Lamb of God, who takes away the sin of the world!'
>
> – JOHN 1:29

The Lamb is a favourite devotional name of Jesus. It signifies the type of man he was when he walked on the earth – gentle and innocent. But more than that, the name is symbolic of deliverance. For the lamb was the most sacred animal offering of the Jewish people. In the well-known Bible story of the Passover, every Jewish family had to put lamb's blood on the doorposts. When the angel of the Lord passed over, killing the firstborn son in every Egyptian home, the blood spared the Jewish families from that death. Just as the Passover lamb freed the Jews from slavery in Egypt, Jesus the Lamb came to free all people from the slavery of sin by his sacrifice on the cross.

Just as I am, without one plea,
But that thy blood was shed for me
And that thou bidst me come to thee
O Lamb of God, I come, I come.

Just as I am, poor, wretched, blind
Sight, riches, healing of the mind
Yea, all I need in thee to find
O Lamb of God, I come, I come.

Just as I am, Thy love unknown
Hath broken every barrier down
Now, to be thine, yea Thine alone,
O Lamb of God, I come, I come.

— CHARLOTTE ELLIOTT

A missionary is one who is wedded to the charter of his Lord and Master; he has not to proclaim his own point of view, but to proclaim the Lamb of God. It is easier to belong to a coterie which tells what Jesus Christ has done for me, easier to become a devotee to Divine Healing, or to a special type of sanctification, or to the baptism of the Holy Ghost. Paul did not say — 'Woe is unto me, if I do not preach what Christ has done for me,' but — 'Woe is unto me, if I preach not the Gospel!' This is the Gospel — 'The Lamb of God, which taketh away the sin of the world!'

— OSWALD CHAMBERS

Who Do You Say I Am?

Little lamb, who made thee?
Dost thou know who made thee,
Gave thee life and bade thee feed
By the stream and o'er the mead;
Gave thee clothing of delight,
Softest clothing, woolly, bright;
Gave thee such a tender voice,
Making all the vales rejoice?
Little lamb, who made thee?
Dost thou know who made thee?

Little lamb, I'll tell thee;
Little lamb, I'll tell thee:
He is called by thy name
For He calls Himself a Lamb,
He is meek, and He is mild,
He became a little child.
I a child and thou a lamb,
We are called by His name.
Little lamb, God bless thee!
Little lamb, God bless thee!

— WILLIAM BLAKE

Your unique tragedy was to do with blood – as I had seen it, peeping in at the local slaughter-house; red and warm and terrible, and at the same time, it seemed, cleansing and sanctifying. Many years after, in Australia, I happened to be present at a sheep shearing. As the lambs looked up with their gentle frightened eyes, it quite often happened that the mechanical shears drew blood. The sight agitated me abnormally – the blood so red against wool so soft and white. Why did I feel as though I had seen it before, long ago? Why was the sight somehow familiar to me? Then my mind went back to the slaughter-house, and to being washed in the blood of the lamb. That was it – the sacrificial lamb. Agnus Dei.

– MALCOLM MUGGERIDGE

O Lord Jesus, Lamb of God,
Bearing such a heavy load;
Pain and suffering was your fate –
Anguish, ridicule and hate.

Tree of anguish, bear my sin;
Heart of Jesus, let me in.
O Lord, may your wounds make whole
Body, spirit and my soul.

– ROBERT CULLINAN

Who Do You Say I Am?

Gentle Jesus, meek and mild,
Look upon a little child,
Pity my simplicity,
Suffer me to come to Thee.

Lamb of God, I look to Thee;
Thou shalt my example be:
Thou art gentle, meek, and mild;
Thou wast once a little child.

Loving Jesus, gentle Lamb,
In Thy gracious hands I am:
Make me, Saviour, what Thou art;
Live Thyself within my heart.

I shall then show forth Thy praise,
Serve Thee all my happy days;
Then the world shall always see
Christ, the holy Child, in me.

— CHARLES WESLEY

Jesus – Always There

M Y name is Hannah and I'm five years old.
I can't see Jesus but I know he's very nice.

He has a smiley, kind face – we can't see it but we just have to know it's smiley.

He's real, not pretend like people on videos.

When you're out shopping with your mummy and you get lost, you can always ask Jesus to help you – and he does.

And when everyone else is being horrid to you in the playground and no one is your friend you can shut your eyes and be friends with Jesus.

He's always there whatever you're doing even when you're all alone.

He can always hear us when we talk to him and we don't have to take it in turns to talk like you do with teachers, because he can hear everyone all at once.

He has cuddles in his heart for everyone but not everyone wants them. Some people don't like Jesus or cuddles.

He loves grown-ups just as much as he loves children, but when anyone is hurt or sad, Jesus looks after them extra carefully.

He makes people better when they are hurt.

Jesus wants us to love people – that makes him happy, but he gets sad when people are horrid and unkind.

When he lived here, people put him on a cross. He didn't stop them because he wanted to take everyone's sins away. When we're naughty we have to say sorry to the person we hurt and if they hurt us we have to forgive them. Then Jesus takes it all away and we can be happy again.

Lord

> At the name of Jesus every knee should bow, in
> heaven and on earth and under the earth, and
> every tongue confess that Jesus Christ is Lord.

– PHILIPPIANS 2:10–11

*Speaking of Jesus as Lord is more than a title of respect, or a
recognition that he is someone to be obeyed. The name Lord
identifies Jesus with his Father, and gives him the right to be
granted the same worship, honour and praise that is offered to
God himself.*

To have a master and to be mastered is not the same thing.
To have a master means that there is one who knows me
better than I know myself, one who is closer than a friend,
one who fathoms the remotest abyss of my heart and
satisfies it, one who has brought me into the secure sense
that he has met and solved every perplexity and problem of
my mind. To have a master is this and nothing less – 'One is
your Master, even Christ.'

Our Lord never enforces obedience; he does not take
means to make me do what He wants. At certain times I
wish God would master me and make me do the thing, but
He will not; in other moods I wish he would leave me alone,
but He does not.

– OSWALD CHAMBERS

Take my life, and let it be
Consecrated, Lord, to Thee.
Take my moments and my days;
Let them flow in ceaseless praise.

Take my hands, and let them move
At the impulse of Thy love.
Take my feet, and let them be
Swift and beautiful for Thee.

Take my voice, and let me sing,
Always, only, for my king.
Take my lips, and let them be
Filled with messages for Thee.

Take my silver and my gold;
Not a mite would I withhold.
Take my intellect, and use
Every power as Thou shalt choose.

Take my will, and make it Thine.
It shall be no longer mine.
Take my heart, it is Thine own;
It shall be Thy royal throne.

Take my love; my Lord, I pour
At Thy feet its treasure-store.
Take myself, and I will be
Ever, only, all for Thee.

— FRANCES RIDLEY HAVERGAL

Who Do You Say I Am?

All hail the power of Jesu's name;
Let angels prostrate fall;
Bring forth the royal diadem
To crown Him Lord of all.

Crown Him, ye martyrs of our God,
Who from His altar call;
Extol Him in whose path ye trod,
And crown Him Lord of all.

Ye seed of Israel's chosen race,
Ye ransomed from the fall,
Hail Him who saves you by His grace,
And crown Him Lord of all.

Sinners! Whose love can ne'er forget
The wormwood and the gall;
Go spread your trophies at His feet,
And crown Him Lord of all.

Let every tribe and every tongue
Before Him prostrate fall,
And shout in universal song
The crownèd Lord of all.

— EDWARD PERRONET

His glory enough to be your servant; it is grace enough that you are my Lord. Jesus, acknowledge what is yours in me and take from me all that is not yours.

— ST BERNARDINE

Lay Thy Hand upon me
When I rashly stray
Into paths forbidden,
Choosing my own way,
Ah! How much correction,
Lord, I have to bear,
Yet must take it meekly,
For Thy Hand is there.

Lead me now and always
Even to the last,
Till the way is ended
And the darkness past:
Till I reach the glory
I was born to share,
This its crown and centre,
That my Lord is there.

— C. M. NOEL

Who Do You Say I Am?

Lord, with what courage and delight
I do each thing,
When Thy least breath sustains my wing!
I shine and move
Like those above,
And, with much gladness
Quitting sadness,
Make me fair days of every night.

Affliction thus mere pleasure is;
And hap what will,
If Thou be in't, 'tis welcome still.
But since Thy rays
In sunny days
Thou thus dost lend,
And freely spend,
Ah! What shall I return for this?

O that I were all soul! That Thou
Wouldst make each part
Of this poor sinful frame pure heart!
Then would I drown
My single one;
And to Thy praise
A concert raise
Of Alleluias here below.

— H. VAUGHAN

The greatest honour a nobleman can bestow upon a poor servant is to treat him as a personal friend, especially if he does it sincerely and wholeheartedly in public and private. The servant will think: 'This high and mighty lord wants to be friends with an ordinary fellow like me – what an honour! He couldn't make me happier if he tried. It's a sight better than giving me hand-outs and looking as if he didn't know me from Adam.'

That is how it is with our Lord Jesus and ourselves. It seems to me that there can surely be no greater joy than that the one who is the most supreme, the most powerful, the finest and best of all, should also be the one who is most lowly, humble, friendly and considerate.

– JULIAN OF NORWICH

Jesus – My Boss

MY name is Bob and I am a carpenter. I think I probably feel closest to Jesus when I'm working – making things, building things, repairing things – after all he was a carpenter too.

Sometimes, when I'm constructing something, I get to a point where I feel totally stuck. I just can't see the best way to do the job, so I stop and ask Jesus, just as if he was my on-site boss, and it always amazes me how the thoughts just come into my head and I see the way to work the problem out.

I've had some horrible bosses in my time, before I became self-employed. You can work all day for them, doing the best you can, then they come round and pick holes in everything, making you feel like dirt.

I really feel Jesus is my boss now. He doesn't just inspect my work at the end of the day, he looks at my heart and sees I've done my best, even if the finished result wasn't quite how it could have been. He sees all the struggles I've had trying to get it right and he's watched the work progress through each stage. There aren't many bosses you'd want *that* close all the time, but Jesus never criticises; you see he understands the job from personal experience. He feels so close I find myself thanking him constantly as each part of the work progresses.

I like to start the day by spending a bit of time with him before leaving for work – plugging my spirit into his. I don't use words, I'm just connecting with him rather than praying – giving him space to come into the ordinary things of my life.

I do a lot of odd jobs for people in their own homes. I often find I'm stuck right in the middle of all their family problems and tensions – a kind of invisible observer – watching children drive mums up the wall, and picking up the uncomfortable feelings between couples. I never interfere but while I'm working, I pray for the whole family, asking Jesus to bring them his peace. Even though I don't talk about him, I've definitely seen his Spirit influencing people as I work and pray for them.

I also love praying for people who are ill, and I am part of my church's prayer ministry team. I have seen people healed and changed through prayer but I do find it hard to understand why Jesus doesn't heal me. I am very deaf and blind in one eye. I became so upset about it recently that, during a service, I told him how angry I was feeling with him. He didn't answer in words, he just showed me a picture of himself holding out his arms. I saw myself running towards him, like a little kid but as I came up close to him I seemed to get lost inside him. Somehow I merged into him, I was still able to see and feel but no one else could see me – all they could see was Jesus. Since then I have continued to feel I am not just with him but *in* him and I am beginning to see people as he sees them and feel about them as he does – particularly the ones who are pressured by worries or in a lot of pain. I just sense how much he loves them, and somehow my own healing doesn't matter so much any more.

Prince of Peace

For to us a child is born, to us a son is given, and
the government will be on his shoulders. And he
will be called Wonderful Counsellor, Mighty God,
Everlasting Father, Prince of Peace.

– ISAIAH 9:6

*Jesus said: 'Peace I leave with you; my peace I give you. I do
not give to you as the world gives' (John 14:27). Only tempor-
ary peace is found in the world. Wars, natural disasters and
crime constantly break into the calm we strive for in our personal
lives. Politicians and New Age gurus make many promises of
peace, but Jesus is the only one who can bring lasting inner
peace and harmony in society.*

Deep peace of the running wave to you
Deep peace of the flowing air to you
Deep peace of the quiet earth to you
Deep peace of the shining stars to you
Deep peace of the son of peace to you.

– CELTIC BLESSING
FROM THE IONA COMMUNITY

Peace, perfect peace, in this dark world of sin?
The blood of Jesus whispers peace within.

Peace, perfect peace, by thronging duties pressed?
To do the will of Jesus, this is rest.

Peace, perfect peace, with sorrows surging round?
Oh Jesus' bosom nought but calm is found.

Peace, perfect peace, with loved ones far away?
In Jesus' keeping we are safe and they.

Peace, perfect peace, our future all unknown?
Jesus, we know, and He is on the throne.

Peace, perfect peace, death shadowing us and ours?
Jesus has vanquished death and all its powers.

It is enough: earth's struggles soon shall cease,
And Jesus call us to heaven's perfect peace.

– EDWARD HENRY BICKERSTETH

To be a fellow son and heir with Christ is healing indeed,
but we have to experience peace with God before we can
know the peace of God.

– BISHOP MORRIS MADDOCKS

Jesus, Lord, we look to thee;
Let in us Thy name agree;
Show Thyself the Prince of Peace,
Bid our strife forever cease.

Make us of one heart and mind,
Gentle, courteous, and kind,
Lowly, meek, in thought and word,
Altogether like our Lord.

Let us for each other care,
Each the other's burdens bear;
To Thy church the pattern give,
Show how true believers live.

Free from anger and from pride;
Let us thus in God abide;
All the depths of love express,
All the heights of holiness.

— CHARLES WESLEY

When Christ came into the world, peace was sung; and when he went out of the world, peace was bequeathed.

— FRANCIS BACON

Drop, drop, slow tears,
And bathe those beauteous feet,
Which brought from heaven
The news and Prince of peace.

Cease not, wet eyes,
His mercies to entreat;
To cry for vengeance
Sin doth never cease.

In your deep floods
Drown all my faults and fears;
Nor let his eye
See sin, but through my tears.

– PHINEAS FLETCHER
17TH-CENTURY POET

Let the peace and quiet of Thy presence take possession of us. Help us to rest, to relax, to become open and receptive to Thee. Thou dost know our innermost spirits, the hidden unconscious life within us, the forgotten memories of hurts and fears, the frustrated desires, the unresolved tensions and dilemmas. Cleanse and sweeten the springs of our being, that freedom, life and love may flow both into our conscious and hidden life. Lord we lie open before Thee, waiting for Thy peace, Thy healing and Thy word. Amen.

– GEORGE APPLETON

Peace is God's direct assurance
To the souls that win release
From this world of hard endurance –
Peace – He tells us – only Peace.

There is Peace in lifeless matter –
There is Peace in dreamless sleep –
Will then Death our being shatter
In annihilation's deep?

Ask you this? O mortal trembler!
Hear the Peace that Death affords –
For your God is no dissembler,
Cheating you with double words:–

To this life's inquiring traveller,
Peace of knowledge of all good:
To the anxious truth-unraveller,
Peace of wisdom understood:–

To the loyal wife, affection
Towards her husband, free from fear,–
To the faithful friend, selection
Of all memories kind and dear:–

To the lover, full fruition
Of an unexhausted joy,–
To the warrior, crowned ambition,
With no envy's base alloy:–

To the ruler, sense of action,
Working out his great intent,—
To the prophet, satisfaction
In the mission he was sent:—

To the poet, conscious glory
Flowing from the Father's face:—
Such is Peace in holy story,
Such is Peace in heavenly grace.

— LORD HOUGHTON

Jesus – A Better Doctor
than I am

MY name is Jenny and I am a single-handed GP in a busy London practice. I'm married with a family.

Ten years ago I felt I had achieved all my goals, my practice was thriving, I had plenty of money and a lovely home. Then suddenly my whole life fell apart when I was diagnosed with breast cancer. Doctors make terrible patients because they know the worst that could happen, and I was very frightened.

Up to that time I only went to church occasionally, but two days before I went into hospital for my mastectomy, our vicar's wife offered to pray for me. I thought, 'I'll have any help that's going', but I have to confess I was a bit put off when she prayed, 'Please Lord, let something really good come out of this situation.' To me, there was nothing 'good' about cancer. But as she continued to pray something definitely happened. I felt a tangible power flowing into me and all the fear vanished. The surgery went perfectly, I had no complications and no post-operative pain. I've had no recurrence of the cancer and have felt fit ever since. I think Jesus reached down, during the vicar's wife's prayer, and healed me, just like he healed people two thousand years ago.

When I was discharged she lent me a little book which explained how Jesus rose from the dead and wants to live by his spirit in our bodies. I went straight up to my bedroom, knelt by my bed and asked him to come into my life and take control of everything.

I soon realised I had been 'taken over' by a far greater doctor than I'll ever be, and I thought, 'This is great! All I'll have to do is sit in my surgery with my feet on the desk and pray for each patient as they come in! Jesus will heal them all, and I won't even have to write out a prescription.' Well, it hasn't worked out like that, because of course not all my patients *want* me to pray with them. If I start they think I must consider them totally beyond medical help! So I've learnt to be a bit more discreet. I do pray for each patient, but under my breath. I am very aware of Jesus, in the surgery with me as I work, guiding me over diagnosis and treatment; giving me his kind of love for people who are, humanly speaking, far from lovable and allowing his power to flow through my hands. I've seen some remarkable things happen: cancers going into remission, depressions lifted and patients with incurable medical conditions begin to recover.

Perhaps one of the greatest things Jesus does is impart his peace to my patients, just as he did for me before my surgery. He doesn't always heal the terminally ill, but he does help them to die well, and with hope. I find that deeply satisfying. He gives *me* his peace too, when I'm under pressure at work – and with the family at home! For me the secret of living in that peace is spending a few minutes alone with Jesus before I leave for work in the morning. I sit in my chair, in the corner of my study and I talk to him about the day ahead and let him talk to me as I read about him in the Bible. Then I let his spirit fill me up all over again before I dash out into the London traffic and the turmoil of a busy day.

Redeemer

> In him we have redemption through his blood, the
> forgiveness of sins, in accordance with the riches
> of God's grace that he lavished on us with all
> wisdom and understanding.

> — EPHESIANS 1:7–8

The practice of redemption is alien to us today, although we might just be familiar with the concept of 'redeeming' a costly item that's been pawned. But in the Greek world redemption meant that slaves were freed by the payment of a ransom. Though slavery is now outlawed in much of the world, many people are still enslaved by sin. Today it is Christ who pays the ransom to free from bondage. He didn't write a cheque, or hand over hard cash. He paid through the shedding of his blood all those years ago.

I know that my redeemer liveth,
and that He shall stand at the latter day upon the earth,
And though worms destroy this body,
Yet in my flesh shall I see God, yet in my flesh shall

I see God.

I know that my redeemer liveth.
For now is Christ risen from the dead,
The first-fruits of them that sleep.

— FROM HANDEL'S *MESSIAH* (JOB 19:25)

My Great Redeemer's Throne

O for a heart to praise my God,
A heart from sin set free,
A heart that always feels Thy blood
So freely spilt for me.

A heart resigned, submissive, meek,
My great Redeemer's throne,
Where only Christ is heard to speak,
Where Jesus reigns alone:

A humble, lowly, contrite heart,
Believing, true, and clean;
Which neither life nor death can part
From Him that dwells within:

A heart in every thought renewed,
And full of love divine;
Perfect, and right, and pure, and good,
A copy, Lord, of Thine.

Thy nature, gracious Lord, impart;
Come quickly from above,
Write Thy new name upon my heart,
Thy new, best name of love. Amen.

— CHARLES WESLEY

The marrow of Job's comfort lies in that little word my – 'my Redeemer' – and in the fact that his Redeemer lives. Oh, to get hold of a living Christ! Certainly if Job, in those ages before the coming of Christ, could say, 'I know,' we should not speak any less positively. A living Redeemer, truly mine, is joy unspeakable.

– CHARLES SPURGEON

> Creator of the starry height,
> Thy people's everlasting Light,
> Jesu, Redeemer of us all,
> Hear thou thy servants when they call.

– 7TH-CENTURY ADVENT OFFICE HYMN

There is only one relationship that matters, and that is your personal relationship to a personal redeemer and Lord. Let everything else go, but maintain that at all costs, and God will fulfil His purpose through your life. One individual life may be of priceless value to God's purposes, and yours may be that life.

– OSWALD CHAMBERS

I am not my own, but the Lord's. He has bought me with a price and I have given myself to him again and again. Therefore I will glorify him with body and soul which are his.

— SIMON PATRICK

Blessed Redeemer, full of compassion,
Great is Thy mercy, boundless and free;
Now in my weakness, seeking Thy favour,
Lord, I am coming closer to Thee.

Blessed Redeemer, wonderful Saviour,
Fountain of wisdom, Ancient of Days,
Hope of the faithful, Light of all ages,
Jesus my Saviour, Thee I will praise.

Blessed Redeemer, gracious and tender,
Now and forever dwell Thou in me;
Thou, my Protector, Shield and Defender,
Draw me and keep me closer to Thee.

— FANNY CROSBY

Jesus – My Hope

Y name is John, I'm in prison, serving a six-year sentence for child sexual abuse. When I first arrived here I felt too numb to feel anything about what I had done. Then I started therapy. It's designed to make us sex offenders realise just how much damage we have done to children and to shock us so thoroughly we never lapse again after release. I began to feel haunted by guilt – I wanted to be punished severely but nothing I went through seemed bad enough to wipe out what I'd done.

I knew all about Jesus – in my head. I used to sing in the church choir when I was a kid, and my wife was always on at me to go with her to church but I was drinking hard and doing things I hated myself for doing.

When I arrived in Dartmoor Prison I felt I'd messed up so badly there was no way back to Jesus – ever. In here sex offenders are the lowest of the low and *child* sex abusers are even lower than that!

Then a group of people from Holy Trinity Church, Brompton, came to talk to us. In a 'bang up' prison, you'll do anything just to get out of your cell for a bit, so I went along. They came to tell us about an *Alpha* course they were going to start, so men could find out what it means to be a Christian. I didn't take much notice until this girl began to sing about Jesus and how he loves people – even people like me. I began to cry – I couldn't stop. When I got back to my cell I put my head in my towel and went on crying so much and for so long that the towel was wringing wet before I finally went to sleep.

I did the *Alpha* course and at the end there was a chance for us to be baptised. Something incredible happened to me that day, I felt I was being washed clean of all that disgusting filth. I could never possibly explain just how much that meant to me.

There's a picture in the prison where I am now, on the way into the chapel. It's of Jesus dying on the cross. Every time I walk past it I want to cry. It makes it all so real – all the agony he went through – so people like me can be clean again. It blows my mind!

But I do still struggle because I know I damaged the child I abused so badly that her life could be scarred for ever. I feel so terrible about that sometimes that I'd willingly be crucified myself, if only I could make it all right for her. But even if I *was* crucified it wouldn't help her. Recently I've come to believe that Jesus can heal emotional scars so I'm praying that he'll do that for her. I would willingly spend the rest of my life trying to help her, but I may never be allowed to communicate with her again in any way. But I believe that Jesus can; I just have to trust him to take care of her and undo the damage I did.

Saviour

We have put our hope in the living God, who is the Saviour of all men, and especially of those who believe.

– I TIMOTHY 4:10

This name is perhaps the best known to all of us – even by those who don't admit to believing. For who, in all honesty, hasn't cried out for him to save when all else has failed? Jesus suddenly becomes real when we see him as our only source of survival – the only one who can rescue us from our particular circumstances. Around the world, Jesus is known as the one who saves, not only from sin, but from all kinds of physical and emotional suffering.

See, oh see, what love the Saviour
Also hath on us bestowed;
How he bled for us and suffered,
How he bare the heavy load.
On the cross and in the garden
Oh how sore was this distress!
Is not this a love that passeth
Aught that tongue can e'er express?

– FRANCES RIDLEY HAVERGAL

Jesu! Bless our slender boat,
By the current swept along;
Loud its threatenings, – let them not
Drown the music of a song
Breathe Thy mercy to implore,
Where these troubled waters roar!

Saviour, for our warning seen
Bleeding on that precious Rood;
If, while thro' the meadows green
Gently wound the peaceful flood,
We forgot Thee, do not Thou
Disregard Thy suppliants now!

– WILLIAM WORDSWORTH

O Saviour Christ, who dost lead them to immortal blessedness, who commit themselves to Thee: Grant that we, being
weak, presume not to trust in ourselves, but may always
have Thee before our eyes, to follow Thee, our guide; that
Thou, who only knowest the way, mayst lead us to our
heavenly desire. To Thee with the Father and the Holy
Ghost be glory for ever.

– PRIMER OF 1559

Who Do You Say I Am?

They promise to erect my royal stem,
To make me great, to advance my diadem,
If I will first fall down, and worship them!

But for refusal they devour my thrones,
Distress my children, and destroy my bones;
I fear they'll force me to make bread of stones.

My life they prize at such a slender rate,
That in my absence they draw bills of hate,
To prove the king a traytor to the State.

Felons obtain more privilege than I,
They are allow'd to answer ere they die;
'Tis death for me to ask the reason why.

But, sacred Saviour, with Thy words I woo
Thee to forgive, and not be bitter to
Such as Thou know'st do not know what they do

– KING CHARLES I
(WRITTEN WHILE IMPRISONED IN CARISBROOKE
CASTLE, 1648. HE WAS CONVICTED OF TREASON
AND EXECUTED THE FOLLOWING YEAR.)

O Saviour, pour upon me thy spirit of meekness and love,
annihilate the selfhood in me, be thou all my life. Guide thou
my hand which trembles exceedly upon the rock of ages.

– WILLIAM BLAKE

One morning I woke with these words on my lips: 'We follow a stripped and crucified Saviour.'

Those words go very deep. They touch everything, one's outer life as well as one's inner: motives, purposes, decisions, everything. Let them be with you. You are sure to have tests as well as many an unexpected joy. But if you follow a stripped and crucified saviour, and by the power of His resurrection seek to enter into the fellowship of His sufferings, you will go on in peace and be one of those blessed ones who spread peace all around.

– AMY CARMICHAEL

The Double Clasp

The Saviour's hand – how close its hold,
That none can loosen, none can break.
No powers of heaven or earth or hell
That loving clasp can ever shake.

And over Jesus' wounded hand
The Father's hand of strength is laid,
Omnipotent to save and keep;
Thus is our surety surer made.

So, one beneath and one above,
Father and Son their hands unite.
How safe, how safe the ransomed are
Within that clasp of tender might!

– ANNIE JOHNSON FLINT

The Last Hour

Be merciful, be gracious, spare him, Lord!
Be merciful, be gracious, Lord, deliver him,
From the sins that are past;
From Thy frown and Thine ire;
From the perils of dying;
From any complying
With sin, or denying
His God, or relying
On self at the last;
From the nethermost fire;
From all that is evil;
From the power of the devil;
Thy servant deliver,
For once and for ever.
By Thy birth and by Thy Cross,
Rescue him from endless loss;
By Thy death and burial,
Save him from a final fall;
By Thy rising from the tomb,
By Thy mounting up above,
By the spirit's gracious love,
Save him in the day of doom.

— ANON

Jesus – My Power to Forgive

MY name is Mary and I am John's wife. The night when I was told that he had been arrested for child sex abuse I felt like a piece of glass which had been dropped and shattered into a thousand pieces. I had already met Jesus by then, and had been praying, for some years, that John would also come to know him. So when I heard about all the terrible things he had been doing in secret, I felt all my hopes were smashed into sharp, jagged fragments. As I lay there in our empty bed, knowing that John was locked in a police cell, I cried out to the Lord in desperation. How could I stay married to a man who could do such things? I think I just wanted to die, but suddenly I definitely felt Jesus was speaking to me, right there in the darkness. He told me to stand by John, and that he could forgive him and wash his sins away.

I really did not think it would ever be possible for *me* to forgive John – ever – but the more I clung to Jesus, during the next horrible months, the more I found he was changing my heart and giving me his power to forgive. When I tried to explain to people that I was going to stand by John, they simply couldn't understand me. Nearly everyone I know, including my relatives and even my Christian friends felt, for the sake of our children, I ought to have nothing more to do with him. If I had not had that 'encounter' with Jesus that first terrible night I am sure I would have taken their advice.

Then, as the time of the trial approached I began to pray constantly, 'Please Jesus, don't let the jury find John guilty, don't let him go to prison.' When my minister gave me this verse – Romans 8:28 – 'And we know that in all things God works for the good of those who love him', I was delighted. I put it up on my kitchen wall, feeling certain that it meant John would be set free, so I was thrown into terrible despair when he was sent to Dartmoor Prison for a six-year sentence. I used to stand in my kitchen, looking at that verse, thinking, 'How could anything good possibly come out of such a mess as this?'

For weeks I felt as if I was being sucked down into a black hole until, one day I was reading my *Daily Bread* Bible reading notes which quoted something Corrie ten Boom once wrote in a Nazi prison camp during World War Two. 'There is no pit so deep that God's love is not deeper still. And there is nothing we do, no matter how stupid, that God cannot make into part of his beauty and purpose.' I was still not sure how God could manage this for our family, but I knew he wanted me to trust him. When John went to that

Alpha course and discovered the forgiveness that is possible through the cross, I began to realise that Jesus really had known what he was doing by allowing John to go to Dartmoor because John has changed so completely since he met Jesus. The difference that I see in him, as I visit him each month, is amazing.

All the time John has been away I have felt Jesus so near to me and the children, providing a home for us, taking care of the bills and keeping us safe in every possible way. Most prisoners' wives find it very difficult, going into the prisons to visit their husbands. There is no privacy and the tense, gloomy prison atmosphere gets to them, making many feel depressed for days afterwards. I have never experienced any of that. I ought also to feel nervous of driving such a long distance on my own, but I find I feel closer to Jesus during the day each month when I visit John than at any other time. He comes with me in the car, stands beside us as we talk and then comforts me on the way home afterwards. It is very strange being married to a man you only see briefly and in public a few times a year. It is also strange being married to someone the world despises and condemns but I know that it is not my own love which I feel towards my husband, it is the love Jesus has given.

Now the time for John's release is drawing near, I must confess that I feel very fearful about our future.

How will our relatives, friends and the local community react to him? Perhaps they will find it very hard to accept him after what he did. I know John has changed, but they may not believe that. Their prejudice may hurt us both very badly, and we may face a lot of problems and loneliness in the future. Yet I know that Jesus can make it possible for us to forgive them. Through all that has happened to us I have discovered that he really can change the way we feel about one another, down here on Earth.

Two in One

SON OF GOD AND SON OF MAN

Then Nathanael declared, 'Rabbi, you are the Son of God; you are the King of Israel.' Jesus said, 'You believe because I told you I saw you under the fig-tree. You shall see greater things than that.' He then added, 'I tell you the truth, you shall see heaven open, and the angels of God ascending and descending on the Son of Man.'

– JOHN 1:49–50

Jesus is referred to as the Son of God – and refers to himself as the Son of Man around eighty times. The name Son of God identifies Jesus with his heavenly father – as an obedient son willing to follow his father's plan for his life. But Jesus was just as keen to identify himself as the Son of Man. Growing up a carpenter, in the house of his earthly parents, he lived a relatively normal life for around thirty years. In the same way, Christians today are both children of their biological parents, and also sons and daughters of the living God, with all the privileges that go with the title.

Never man spoke like this Man
And he spoke His word to me:
Never man loved like this Man
And His love reached down to me:
Never man gave like this Man
And He gave His life for me:
Never man lived like this Man lives,
And He shares His life with me!

– CATHERINE BRAMWELL-BOOTH

God sent His Son, they called Him Jesus;
He came to love, heal and forgive;
He lived and died to buy my pardon,
An empty grave is there to prove my saviour lives.

Because He lives I can face tomorrow;
Because He lives all fear is gone;
Because I know He holds the future,
And life is worth the living
Just because He lives.

– WILLIAM J. GAITHER

On the Mount of Ascension the transfiguration was completed, and our Lord went back to his primal glory; but he did not go back simply as Son of God: he went back as Son of Man as well as Son of God. That means there is freedom of access now for anyone straight to the very throne of God through the ascension of the Son of Man. At his ascension our Lord entered heaven, and he keeps the door open for humanity to enter.

— OSWALD CHAMBERS

The Jesus who emerges from the Gospels is this man who tells me, who explains to me, the ways of God, and, I also think, who explains to God the ways of man. In other words, he is an intermediary between God and men who reveals in his person and in his life the unity that we have sensed, and who translates it into individual terms.

— MALCOLM MUGGERIDGE

Now the Son, true God and true Man, can sit peacefully and quietly in his city which God planned should be his before time began; and the Father is in the Son and the Holy Spirit is in the Father and in the Son.

— JULIAN OF NORWICH

Two suns appear to men to-day: one made,
One maker: one eternal, one to fade,
One the Stars' King; the King of their King, one:
This makes – that bids him make – the hours to run.
The Sun shines with the True Sun, ray with ray,
Light with light, Day with Him that makes the day.
Day without night, without seed bears the fruit,
Unwedded mother, Flower without a root.
She than all greater: He the greatest still;
She filled by Him whose glories all things fill.
That night is almost day, and yields to none,
Wherein God flesh, wherein flesh God, put on.
The undone is done again; attuned the jar:
Sun precedes day, the morn, the morning star.
True Sun, and Very Light, and Very Day:
God was that Sun, and God its Light and ray.
How bare the Virgin, ask'st Thou, God and Man?
I know not: but I know God all things can.

– ST HILDEBERT

TRANSLATED BY JOHN MASON NEALE

Who Do You Say I Am?

O Christ, Son of the living God,
May your holy angels guard our sleep.
May they watch us as we rest
And hover around our beds.

Let them reveal to us in our dreams
Visions of your glorious truth,
O High Prince of the universe,
O High Priest of the mysteries.

May no dreams disturb our rest
And no nightmares darken our dreams.
May no fears or worries delay
Our willing, prompt repose.

May the virtue of our daily work
Hallow our nightly prayers.
May our sleep be deep and soft,
So our work be fresh and hard.

– EVENING HYMN
ATTRIBUTED TO ST PATRICK

Jesus – All I Need

MY name is Jen and I'm a writer. During the eight years I spent confined to a wheelchair by a crippling neurological illness, I had a very special experience of Jesus. We were on holiday in Devon and one morning, as I sat by the sea, I was suddenly aware of Jesus standing on a rock, close beside me. All I could see was his outline but I felt a strong sense of his presence. I began to ask him why he had not healed me, after so many agonised prayers, but he didn't answer. So I asked him for spiritual gifts so that I could serve him better – from my wheelchair – but suddenly his voice cut into my whinging requests. Distinctly I heard him say, 'All you need is me.'

But what does that mean? He has been many things to me at various stages of my life. I've related to him via most of the biblical models. He's been a father, master, friend, shepherd, brother, king, healer, but I think it is only when we have nothing else but him that we discover he really is all we need.

I was lucky enough to have parents who loved me, an adoring granny, a brother who was my best friend, a husband, who for thirty years loved me devotedly and six children who returned my love most satisfactorily.

You feel so safe and protected in a warm cotton wool covering like that, but life has a brutal way of ripping off those cosy layers. Eventually we all lose the people we love – they die, reject us, grow up, leave home, become ill, old or senile.

One day, after my parents were dead, my brother had moved to the far side of the world and the last of my children had gone to university, my husband told me he had someone else, and left to live with her.

The sense of abandonment was terrible.

At that moment I didn't need Jesus to be a distant deity wagging a disapproving finger at my failure and stupidity. I didn't need a master, a dad or a friend. During the long, sleepless nights I realised that, throughout the Bible, we are given a far more intimate way of relating to him – as a lover, bridegroom and husband. It dawned on me that the biblical 'husband' was responsible for meeting his wife's needs – both practical and emotional; his role was to cherish, protect and provide for her all the days of her life – in fact to love her as he loved his own body (Ephesians 5:28).

At that loneliest point in my life, I realised Jesus wanted to be that kind of a husband for me. All my props were gone, all I had left was him, so was it true that he was all I needed?

When other people, or our own abilities, are no longer meeting our emotional or practical needs (and this can happen at any stage in life), we can either drown in despair or we can look towards Jesus, by faith and allow him to meet the shortfall. The more frightening life feels, the more he is able to be our protector. When we are helpless and weak, he can become our strength. When we are punch-drunk by the unkindness of others, he can be our comfort; confused by life, he becomes our wisdom. In short our pain, loneliness and failure release his supernatural power in our lives.

Jesus is not merely a Zimmer frame for broken-hearted cripples. It's just that youth, strength and success fool us into thinking we can manage without him. Life equals loss and the more we lose in earthly terms the more we can 'find' Jesus. And when our need for him is paramount that is when we *really* know him.

Sometimes when I see couples of my age holding hands, sharing jokes, enjoying each other, it hurts like a stab in the stomach but if I turn, by faith, to my 'new husband' and take his hand then joy replaces the pain. The same applies when bills arrive which I can't pay or I wake alone and frightened in the night. He was right when he said, 'All you need is me', and now I've proved it.

God

In the beginning was the Word, and the Word was with God, and the Word was God. He was with God in the beginning. Through him all things were made; without him nothing was made that has been made. In him was life, and that life was the light of men. The light shines in the darkness, but the darkness has not understood it.

The true light that gives light to every man was coming into the world. He was in the world, and though the world was made through him, the world did not recognise him. He came to that which was his own, but his own did not receive him. Yet to all who received him, to those who believed in his name, he gave the right to become children of God – children born not of natural descent, nor of human decision or a husband's will, but born of God. The Word became flesh and made his dwelling among us. We have seen his glory, the glory of the One and Only, who came from the Father, full of grace and truth.

No-one has ever seen God, but God the One and Only, who is at the Father's side, has made him known.

– JOHN 1:1–5, 9–14, 18

He is the image of the invisible God, the firstborn over all creation. For by him all things were created: things in heaven and on earth, visible and invisible, whether thrones or powers or rulers or authorities; all things were created by him and for him. He is before all things, and in him all things hold together. And he is the head of the body, the church; he is the beginning and the firstborn from among the dead, so that in everything he might have the supremacy. For God was pleased to have all his fullness dwell in him, and through him to reconcile to himself all things, whether things on earth or things in heaven, by making peace through his blood, shed on the cross.

– COLOSSIANS 1:15–20

In the past God spoke to our forefathers through the prophets at many times and in various ways, but in these last days he has spoken to us by his Son, whom he appointed heir of all things and through whom he made the universe. The Son is the radiance of God's glory and the exact representation of his being, sustaining all things by his powerful word. After he had provided purification for sins, he sat down at the right hand of the Majesty in heaven.

– HEBREWS 1:1–3